GANGBUSTER

Tales of the Old Grey Fox

D1639284

GANGBUSTER

Tales of the Old Grey Fox

Bert Wickstead

Futura

A Futura Book

First published in Great Britain in 1985 by
Futura Publications, a Division of
Macdonald & Co (Publishers) Ltd
London & Sydney

ISBN 0 7088 2478 1

Photoset in North Wales by
Derek Doyle & Associates, Mold, Clwyd.
Reproduced, printed and bound in Great Britain by
Hazell Watson & Viney Limited,
Member of the BPCC Group,
Aylesbury, Bucks

Futura Publications
A Division of
Macdonald & Co (Publishers) Ltd
Maxwell House
74 Worship Street
London EC2A 2EN

A BPCC plc Company

I dedicate this book, firstly to all my friends and ex-colleagues who helped to make it possible.

Also, and in particular, to my dear wife Jean, for her patience and cheerful encouragement over long hours of duty, and the anxieties associated with them.

Contents

Contents

CHAPTER ONE

THE TWILIGHT WORLD

Pride of place in my living room belongs to a chair. To you, it might seem a very ordinary sort of chair. But to me, it will always be special because so many of my memories are wrapt around it. A brass plate carries the words, 'This is the hot seat from which all the big decisions were taken.' It is, in fact, my farewell gift from the force – the chair I used as commander of the Serious Crime Squad, the aptly-named 'Untouchables'.

Now I only have to sit in this chair, close my eyes, and the memories of a strange and different world come flooding back; the gangland world of kidnappings, beatings and contract killings; the twilight world of blue movies, vice lords and Mayfair madams; the fantasy world of the villains in which nicknames such as The Undertaker, The Landlord, Little Caesar and The Godfather come to sound almost commonplace.

I see again the women who thread their way through my story: the beautiful prophetess of a master race, Françoise Jordan; call girl Norma Levy who rocked a government; and Fay Sadler with her gangster lovers and ill-fated affairs.

From the backrooms of my mind come the courtroom scenes as sentences are passed: the Dixons' threat, 'Wickstead, we will get you'; the promise of Selwyn Cooney's father, 'My son's death won't go unavenged'; and Syndicate boss Bernie Silver's mock bow to me from the dock of the Old Bailey.

I could begin the book with each and every one. But

because this is intended to be a simple story, it is perhaps best to begin the simplest way of all … at the beginning.

CHAPTER TWO

ON THE BEAT

'Are you all right? What have they done to you?'
The first words from police officers who had rushed to the scene of a reported attack on a young policeman named Bert Wickstead.

It was one of those family reunions so beloved by East Enders such as I. Four generations of Wicksteads were gathered under the same roof. The men of the tribe tended to be burly rather than tall, broad of shoulder, deep of chest. The Wickstead women were fashioned along equally generous lines, with ruddy complexions and tranquil minds.

But in that gathering, one man stood out from the rest: my uncle Jack Wickstead, a Detective Sergeant at Chiswick. He was the accepted leader of the Wickstead clan. A big, calm, fearless fellow – honest and straight as ever a man could hope to be. In those immediate post-war years, police officers in London were looked upon as men of respect. And certainly I respected Jack Wickstead. He was my ideal, very much the sort of man I wanted to be. He had just asked me casually enough about my plans for the future – doubtless well aware of the fact that since leaving the army, I had been moving from job to job like a gipsy on the run.

I told him, 'The trouble is that I don't really know what I want to do. I think I may go back into the army. I was happy there.'

'Why?' he asked. 'Why were you happy in the army?'

I hadn't given it much thought before. I said, 'I suppose it was mainly the comradeship. I enjoyed being part of a team, of feeling that maybe we were doing something worthwhile.'

He nodded as though he understood. 'You know,' he said, 'you just might find the same sort of pleasure in police work. Sleep on it. Give it some thought. And if you want to take it a step further, let me know.'

He was wise enough to leave it there. But all of a sudden I knew I didn't really need to sleep upon it at all. No doubt about it, this was what I wanted to do. I was surprised it had taken me so long to find out.

However, that enthusiasm was almost still-born – the career of the future Gangbuster was nearly over before it had begun. I failed my eyesight test at the all-important medical. But at that crucial moment in my life, I noticed that the officer in charge of us was looking at his list in a thoughtful sort of way. He looked at me. 'Wickstead,' he said. 'That's an unusual name. You wouldn't by any chance have a relative in the force, would you?'

I told him that my uncle was a Detective Sergeant at Chiswick. He nodded slowly. 'Jack Wickstead,' he said, 'A good man. Is that the one?'

I said, 'Yes, that's the one.'

'In that case,' he said promptly, 'let's take that test again.' This time, mercifully, I scraped through.

My first station was Hampstead where I fell into the very good hands of what we would have termed in the army a band of 'old sweats': Jack Beaumont, Dinger Bell, Sailor Knight, Bert Fowler and Dutchy Holland. All characters in their own right. None of them perfect. In their composite form, they were the epitome of the British bobby. And in my book, that makes them the salt of the earth. Certainly they were easy men to remember.

Jack Beaumont was a tall, lugubrious, cadaverous looking gent, very affable and ever ready to impart knowledge to a new recruit such as I. Many years later, he became a coroner's officer. With those cadaverous features, he could have been typecast for such a role.

Dinger Bell was a loner, an old, single PC who tended to talk in grunts and monosyllables. On the rare

11

occasions when he did string an entire sentence together, he was worth listening to. He had a fetish about wearing a woolly cardigan under his tunic. He'd once caught pneumonia and was quite determined not to repeat the experience. Above all else, he was a prodigious drinker of tea. Living alone in police accommodation, above the station, the force had become his family. Even on his off-duty nights, he would haunt the station, inevitably clutching his most cherished possession, an old aluminium tea pot. I shared a lot of beats with Dinger and amongst other things he taught me where best to get a hot cup of tea on a cold night. To a bobby on the beat, that can be a prize beyond pearls.

Sailor Knight, as his name suggests, had served in the Merchant Navy. He walked with a nautical roll. He even had bow legs. By police standards, he was small; but a busy little man, always on the move. He did a lot of work with the Police Federation and gave us young PCs much good advice about pensions and the like. But Sailor's grand passion was cricket. Even in the station, if you watched him closely you would see his arms move in strange mysterious ways as he played the classic cover drive or bowled the unplayable ball.

Bert Fowler was my first section sergeant. A former army sergeant-major who looked the part, he was tall, well-built, ramrod straight and possessed of a magnificent military moustache waxed at the ends. But behind that fierce exterior there beat a heart of gold. There was even a touch of the mother hen in Bert as he looked after and worried about his chicks – the young PCs. He would make a point of finding you on your beat and having a quiet, friendly word. An entirely likeable man in every respect.

Dutchy Holland was a great big bear of a fellow – six feet five and built like a tank. A nice man who worked at his own pace which was deceptively slow and leisurely. Everyone in the neighbourhood knew Dutchy. He was an institution. They knew too that although he was easy-going, ever ready for a laugh, you must never take liberties with Dutchy. If he so much as wagged his big finger at you, it was time to listen. And rather carefully.

I have good reason to be grateful to them all. Five old sweats who really knew the ropes and still had the time and the patience to pass on their knowledge to a new recruit. Mind you, they never had a better listener. I wanted to learn every single thing there was to know about the job. I was very ambitious and the first step in those ambitions was to get into the CID. So I set out to catch thieves and assorted villains, knowing that the more arrests I put on my record, the sooner I would achieve that initial dream.

Sometimes I was a little too keen for my own good. I badgered my inspector for permission to attend a post-mortem, considering this an essential experience for any would-be CID officer. Finally my wish was granted. Now if I had been a bit older, a bit wiser, I might have been content to view the proceedings from a distance. But eager to learn, to understand everything that was happening, I pushed my way to the front. No one made any attempt to stop me. Then all of a sudden the room started to sway. Next thing I remember was finding myself sitting on the front steps of the mortuary out in the cool air. The waxed moustache and the anxious eyes of Bert Fowler were hovering over me. It wasn't the sight that had caused this. It never is. It was the smell.

Another over-eager moment came with the collapse and death of a man on Hampstead Heath. By the time I arrived, the inevitable small crowd of onlookers had gathered. I pushed my way through and, anxious to show initiative, held a small mirror to the lips of what was already a corpse. I had doubtless seen too many detective movies.

Later Bert Fowler delivered a quiet little homily. 'Lad,' he said, 'it's best to leave that sort of caper to the doctor. The English don't like to make a public spectacle of death. The English like to die privately.'

Still, by far and away my most embarrassing moment arrived on a Saturday morning in Kilburn High Road, a

13

favoured haunt of the barrow boys. One of the fraternity was quite clearly obstructing the pavement. He had been told to move along and had made no effort to do so. Yet although Dutchy Holland was looming large, nothing had been done about this. I found this puzzling. So eventually I told him once more to move and when he refused, I arrested him, with every intention of taking him down to the station.

'What happens to the barrow?' he asked. 'If we leave it there, everything on it will get nicked.'

'Well, you'd better push it,' I replied.

He was clearly better versed in this section of the law than yours truly. 'Oh no,' he said. 'Now that I'm an arrested person, all I have to do is walk along peacefully beside you. As the arresting officer, you are responsible for the safety of my property. And that means that you do the pushing.'

He was, of course, quite right. I pushed the barrow all the way to the station, doing my best to ignore the ironic chorus of 'Ripe bananas' as we marched along the road with Dutchy alongside with my prisoner, holding an animated discourse on football.

That night Dutchy lectured me in that slow, deliberate way of his, spacing out each word. 'My son,' he said, 'if you had contained yourself, I would have explained to you the pitfalls of arresting barrow boys on a Saturday morning.

'It's a bloody different kettle of fish between when they're setting out their stalls in the morning and when they're packing up at night. Now that is the time to nick them – not when their barrows are full. So, my son, if you wish to become a good officer, you must first learn to curb your impetuosity.' One of the finest object lessons I ever learned.

Still there were credits too. For instance, my first major arrest – a beacon in any policeman's life. It was close to midnight and I was standing in the entrance to the Hampstead underground station. The rain had gone away, but the streets were quieter than usual. Then a man came walking by, carrying a case. He was spotlighted for a moment under a street lamp, a tall, well-built fellow with a slightly shifty manner. He was wearing a dry overcoat over soaking wet trousers. It didn't make a lot of sense. So I stopped him and asked to see what he was carrying in his case at this late hour.

He shrugged with the resignation of the old lag. 'All right, it's a fair cop,' he said. He too had obviously seen too many detective movies. He opened the case. It was filled with silver and jewellery, the proceeds of three burglaries committed that night.

I arrested him and as we walked towards the station, he couldn't have been more docile. Another PC joined us and we strolled along with chummy between us. Then just fifty yards away from the station, the docility departed. He swung the case at me and next moment the two of us were rolling around on the pavement. A few minutes later, after a rough-and-tumble, I regained the upper hand. But looking up, I spotted my fellow PC leaning against the wall, having watched the fight with interest and – judging by his smile – some amusement.

'Thanks for the help,' I said.

He was in no way abashed. 'You didn't need any help,' he said. 'You were doing all right on your own.'

To be fair, he had a point. When two police officers try to subdue a prisoner, they can all too easily get in one another's way.

However, the event at Hampstead which made the most lasting impression came one night when I stopped an army truck. All I had intended to do was tell them that one of their sidelights wasn't working. But before I could say anything, five soldiers jumped out of the back of the truck and started running. I had no idea what this was all about, but I meant to find out. I grabbed one of them and shouted as his companions disappeared into the darkness. The street was dimly lit and someone watching from a house nearby clearly got the wrong impression. They heard my shout, saw my uniform and the milling group, then dialled 999. Out went the call: 'Police officer

15

is being attacked by five men. In need of assistance.'

Suddenly squad cars were arriving from all directions and the area was full of policemen. Sailor Knight was the first to reach me. His opening words: 'Are you all right? What have they done to you?' And that thought was echoed by them all. I was discovering how the police look after their own – and it's a moment I shall never forget. If I'd ever had the slightest doubt concerning my choice of a career, it was washed away that night. I was where I wanted to be and where I intended to stay. Incidentally, the five soldiers had stolen cases of butter from the local barracks. They were all caught and convicted at a court-martial.

Soon after this, I was transferred to Harrow Road as a detective constable. The first part of my ambitions had been achieved. But due to an unfortunate set of circumstances, my stay was to be a very brief one.

A man had been arrested in Ennis, County Clare, for a job I was investigating. So I flew out to Eire with an aide, Sam Glendenning, to escort him back to London. It was February and by the time we reached Dublin, the weather had closed in. With visibility down to fifty yards, all inland flights had been cancelled. So Aer Lingus provided us with a car to take us to Ennis. It was a nightmare journey, made worse by the fact that I was feeling rough, and not understanding the reason why. We arrived in Ennis late at night and found the local Guarda office deserted. However, we were directed to a hostelry where some seventy people, including the Guarda, were drinking in front of beautiful open fires. We couldn't have been made more welcome. Glasses were thrust into our hands, our shoulders were patted and everyone wanted to say hello. It should have been the beginning of a memorable night, but sadly I wasn't in the mood. I was feeling terrible. So I made my excuses and staggered off to bed.

I awoke in the early evening of the following day. I was in hospital with a doctor, a nurse, a Guarda officer, a black-robed priest and a worried-looking Sam all

16

grouped around my bed. I had gone down with a particularly bad case of quinsy; and several weeks would go by before I was fit enough to be discharged.

Once I was well enough to take an interest in the world around me, I found the experience quite amusing. Every night, the wives of my fellow patients would arrive. The ritual never changed. As befitted good Catholics, they would produce their beads and say their 'Hail Mary's.' Then, at a given signal, out would come the whisky and the brandy bottles. It was like a conjuring act. And being the hospitable people that they were, I would always be included in the drinking party. You just couldn't have found nicer or kinder folk anywhere on earth.

The upshot of all this was that soon after my return to England, the Metropolitan Police were presented with a bill for three thousand pounds – my medical expenses. Eire didn't have a National Health Service. The powers that be were scarcely overjoyed. No one at Harrow Road actually blamed me for catching quinsy. Just the same, there was a feeling that they couldn't really afford to have a young DC with such an apparent propensity for trouble. No tears were shed when I moved rather rapidly to Caledonian Road – in those days, one of the roughest and toughest of all the London beats. It was an area in which you needed to get to know your villains in a hurry. And you can believe me, we had a few!

For a start, there was Billy Hill, then at the very height of his powers. He had a small army of violent men at his beck and call. But he achieved his eminence in the underworld mainly by the use of a rare criminal intelligence. He was cleverer than his rivals. His organisation matched that of the average captain of industry.

Another celebrated villain was Ruby Sparks, who had some newspaper shops in the area. He wasn't quite the rascal he had been. He was moving into maturity, a dry wit who wouldn't indulge in mindless violence. I must confess to having a soft spot for Ruby.

And then there was Freddie Andrews, who owned a

greengrocer's shop at The Rise in Hornsey. Very definitely in the top league of villains. The first time I met Freddie, I arrested him, which is, I suppose, one way to get introduced to a man. He was on our wanted list following a break-in. He had been spotted wheeling a safe away on a wheelbarrow, and had promptly gone on the run.

Then one day I was returning from Bow Street. I stepped on the tube train and there was Freddie Andrews with some of his pals. I recognised him solely from the description given to me by fellow officers. If I'd had any doubts, they would have been dispelled by the actions of his companions. They recognised me and scattered at some speed. Freddie stayed where he was, so I sat down beside him.

I said, 'I believe you to be Freddie Andrews and if so you are wanted at Caledonian Road. I am at Caledonian Road, so let's keep this on a friendly basis and we'll get off the train together.'

He just shrugged his shoulders and said, 'Yep, okay.'

When we reached Caledonian Road, we went up in the lift together. I told the liftman to keep the gates closed and slip across the road to the police station – which was immediately opposite the underground – to fetch some assistance as I had a prisoner.

Freddie turned to me. 'You know, you've no need to do that,' he said. 'I'll walk across the road with you.'

I told him, 'No, Fred. There was no way out while we were together in the tube. But once we're in the street, it's a different matter. So I'd rather you stayed here with me – and we'll still keep it on that friendly basis.'

And that's what we did. He was duly charged and the investigation was then taken out of my hands. I was considered to be a little bit too junior, too inexperienced, to handle a case involving one of London's top villains.

It was disappointing, but I was still confident that my day would come.

CHAPTER THREE

THE PEN CLUB MURDER

'I am the boss of the underworld,' claim by Johnny Nash.

In the early hours of Sunday morning, the 7th of February, 1960, Selwyn Keith Cooney, a front man for the self-described 'King of the Underworld', Billy Hill, was shot to death in the Pen Club, a squalid drinking den in London's East End. The case that followed would highlight the arrogance of the gangs, who had clearly come to believe that they were above and beyond the reach of the law.

Some two hours after the shot had been fired, the phone rang in the hallway of my house. The message was terse. 'This is Commercial Street. Get in here as fast as you can. We have a major incident.'

As always I had moved quickly in the hope that my wife and young son wouldn't be woken. But the wives of policemen tend to wake very easily. When I returned to the bedroom my wife was already sitting up, offering to get me something to eat. One of the odd facets of the job is that when the emergency calls come through, hunger goes away. Yet as soon as you arrive at the station and discover what has to be done, you become voracious. At Commercial Street on such days, there would be a sudden flurry of orders for bacon and saveloy sandwiches and a junior PC would be despatched to one of the takeaway cafes that dotted the area.

I left the house at four o'clock. It was dark on the streets, and cold. London at that time on a Sunday morning can be a very lonely place. I didn't own a car and normally I would have ridden my bicycle to the station. But I was suffering from one of the plagues of mankind, a boil on my backside, and so a bike ride didn't appeal. I walked up to the main road, spotted a PC from Holloway and explained that I was needed at the station.

'No problem, mate,' he said and suiting action to words, he stepped into the road, held up his hand and stopped a newspaper van. 'This officer is wanted at Commercial Street nick in a hurry,' he said. 'Take him!'

The driver, fortunately an equable sort of chap, proceeded to do just that. Commercial Street had been the hub of the Jack the Ripper enquiries and the passing years had done little to change it. Every time I walked in, I half expected to see behind the desk a fat Victorian bobby with one of those waxed moustaches turned up at the end and to hear the words, 'Yes, young sir, and what can I do for you?'

I was one of the first to arrive, but in no time at all the station was a hive of activity. John Bliss, the area chief superintendent, was organising the operation. But Detective Superintendent Roland 'Roly' Millington was in charge of the murder investigation.

When John Bliss saw me moving painfully up the stairs, he asked me what was the matter. I told him and he shrugged. 'You won't be much use to me out on the streets today,' he said. 'Do you reckon you can run the office?' I said I could and he smiled, noting my eagerness.

The boil which I'd been cursing for days had proved to be the proverbial blessing in disguise. As a very junior sergeant, I would normally have played a relatively minor role in the case. But in running the office (or to be more precise, the incident room) I would have a wonderful opportunity to see how a murder investigation was planned and operated. I would learn lessons on this case which would prove invaluable to me in the years ahead.

I had never met Cooney in life. My first sight of him was on the mortuary slab. But we knew a great deal about him. He had been part of a middle-class family in Leeds; and was known variously as Jimmy Neill and 'Little Jimmy', although he was anything but little. He was a six-footer and a very powerfully built man. He had been the manager of the New Cabinet Club in Gerrard Street, Soho, a club almost certainly owned and controlled by Billy Hill. Cooney served as the perfect front man. A handsome man with considerable charm and yet quite capable of taking care of any trouble that might arise. Not a man to be intimidated easily. He was on friendly terms with many of his wealthy Mayfair neighbours and during the day he was often seen exercising his boxer dog in Hyde Park.

At first sight, this might have appeared to be a relatively simple case. Two of Cooney's friends, Joan Bending and Johnny Simons, accompanied his body to the hospital. And outraged by his death, both spoke freely when first questioned by police officers.

In their statements, they explained how Cooney had closed the New Cabinet Club late on the Saturday night and then driven them the two miles across London to the Pen Club in Duval Street, Stepney. Duval Street had been the scene of Jack the Ripper's last recorded murder (that of Mary Jane Kelly in 1888) and it provided a fitting backcloth for a club that was inhabited almost exclusively by criminals and prostitutes. It's possible that a few honest citizens may have crossed its threshold from time to time. But if so, I can only say they were rash to do so; for this was a lawless place. It had changed hands only three weeks before the murder and even the name was believed to be an underworld joke: the club was reputed to have been purchased on the proceeds of a major robbery at the Parker Pen Company. Police had raided the club twice in the previous week and another raid had already been planned.

When Cooney's party arrived, both floors of the club were crowded. The juke box was blaring and the drink was flowing. Fay Sadler, a long-time associate of gangsters, was serving behind the bar. She was officially the manageress and some people referred to it as 'Fay's Club'. The true owners were Billy Ambrose and Jeremiah Callaghan. Both were serving ten-year sentences at the time; but thanks to the benefits of the prison parole system they were allowed to come home each weekend. On that night Ambrose, a former boxer, was acting as doorman-cum-bouncer and Callaghan was mixing with the clients.

Soon after the arrival of Cooney, James Laurence 'Jimmy' Nash, a member of the notorious Nash family, walked into the club. He was accompanied by his girl friend, club hostess Doreen 'Redhead' Masters, and two former professional boxers, Joseph Henry Pyle and John Alexander Read. According to witnesses, Masters said something to Nash and pointed towards Cooney. Nash's face became 'very stern' and he immediately approached Cooney and struck him in the face with an object never identified. The blow broke Cooney's nose and blood gushed freely. Nash was heard to say, 'That will teach you to give little girls a spanking.' Cooney replied that he didn't know what he was talking about. He had never hit a girl in his life. Nash, aided by Read and Pyle, continued to rain blows upon the unfortunate Cooney who fought back as best he could.

Then Mrs Betty Ambrose called out, 'He's got a gun.' And at her shout, there was panic on the crowded floor with men and women struggling to get away from the fighting group. Mrs Ambrose's husband, Billy, immediately left the door and pushed his way through the crowd in a bid to secure the gun. Both Bending and Simons were adamant that it was Nash who had the gun and that he first shot Ambrose in the stomach at almost point-blank range, then turned and shot Cooney in the head. According to the pathologist, Cooney must have died instantly; but he nevertheless staggered across the floor before collapsing over a television set, a happening that caused Joan Bending to believe that he was still alive. Some of the crowd then turned upon Nash and his companions. Simons struck Read over the head with a bottle, splitting his scalp. The Nash faction fled down the stairs under a hail of bottles and glasses.

Nash was driven away from the club by Pyle, while

Doreen Masters departed in another car with the injured Read. Within a minute, the club was deserted. The wounded Billy Ambrose carried Cooney's body down the stairs with the help of Callaghan and Simons. They placed him on the pavement edge some distance from the club. Bending and Simons stayed with the body until the ambulance arrived. Fay Sadler made an attempt to remove all traces of the fight. With the assistance of another woman, she washed away the bloodstains, cleared up the broken glasses and threw a spent cartridge case into a pile of rubbish. Meanwhile Ambrose had gone home, examined his wound, realised it was serious and then driven himself to the London Hospital where he underwent an emergency operation. He stated that he had been shot outside an unknown Paddington club.

Later that same day we were even supplied with a motive for the shooting which, if true, must rate as one of the strangest I ever heard in a murder case. A few weeks earlier, Cooney had been involved in a collision while driving his Vauxhall Victor in Hyde Park. The other driver was the girl friend of Ronnie Nash, one of Jimmy's seven brothers. She was a prostitute known as 'Blonde Vicky'. She admitted that it was her fault, but explained that she had a problem. She wasn't insured. So she suggested that Cooney should get his car repaired and send her the bill. The bill came to 54s 9d (£2.74 in modern currency), but she didn't pay. Then the night before the murder, Cooney met her by chance in a Notting Hill drinking club. She was with Ronnie Nash. Words were exchanged. Nash and two of his followers then attacked Cooney, who gave back rather more than he received. One report stated that he floored Nash with a left hook.

This was the reason, said our informants, why some twenty-four hours later Jimmy Nash set out to avenge his brother's pride. Yet I still find it difficult to believe that a man died for such a petty cause. I don't doubt the basic story. We checked it out very carefully. But I think it much more likely that the incident served as a cloak to disguise the real purpose behind the attack, namely gang warfare. The London underworld of the day was in a state of turmoil. Billy Hill had for long been regarded as the major force. On one occasion when asked to name his occupation in court, he had actually replied, 'I am the king of the underworld.' Although the remark wasn't taken too seriously by counsel, it nevertheless contained an element of truth. Throughout the Fifties, Hill had indeed led the most powerful and best organised of all the London gangs. But now new bands of thugs – notably the Nashes, backed by the Kray twins – were challenging Hill's supremacy. John 'Peacemaker' Nash had been quoted in *The People* newspaper as saying, 'I am now the boss of the underworld.' So the chance quarrel with Hill's front man Cooney may have been viewed as an opportunity to underline that claim.

Now as I was saying, at first sight this might have appeared to be a relatively simple case. And it probably would have been just that, if the shooting had taken place in front of honest, upright citizens. But in such a haunt of criminals as the Pen Club, we were all too well aware of the problems. The underworld, regardless of factions, would close ranks against us.

It was the two hospitals concerned who first informed us about the wounding of Billy Ambrose and the murder of Selwyn Cooney. After that, events moved rapidly. Jeremiah Callaghan and his friend, William Hobbs, returned to Duval Street out of a sense of morbid curiosity. They were recognised and stopped by a very astute police officer. When asked to explain the bloodstains on their clothing, they said that they had been involved in a brawl outside a public house in Walworth, the stamping ground of the Callaghans. Round about the same time, Fay Sadler was spotted leaving the London Hospital in the company of Patrick Callaghan, brother to Jeremiah. When questioned by police, she said she had simply called to see her friend Billy Ambrose and knew nothing at all about the

24

shooting. She gave her name as Mrs Patrick Callaghan and was allowed to proceed upon her way.

Soon after that, Joan Bending and Johnny Simons were brought into Commercial Street for questioning. Joan Bending worked as a barmaid at the New Cabinet Club and had been Cooney's lover. She was nineteen, dark, slim, attractive and in a highly emotional state. The shooting had left her numb, but now the truth was finally beginning to sink in. Selwyn Cooney was dead. Very dead. And her dreams of a future spent with that big and handsome man were dead too. In the strange way of the world, her grief and outrage were turned against the police, her natural allies in this cause at least. 'You are all bastards,' she cried and threatened to throw herself out of the first-floor window.

In her chosen environment, she had needed to grow up quickly. But that hard-won sophistication wasn't proof against something so close as this, the brutal death of a lover. And for a long time, her cries and screams echoed around the station. Yet despite the tears, her intention never wavered. She was determined to give evidence against the men responsible for Cooney's death.

Johnny Simons appeared to be equally determined. He was a small-time crook, a bit of a Jack the lad who enjoyed the bright lights and the company of women. It was easy to see why he had been attracted by Cooney, a playboy with a certain sense of style, the kind of man that Simons wanted to be. But as we were to discover, there was a trace of something worthwhile lurking beneath the somewhat flashy exterior of Simons. When put to the test, he didn't lack courage.

A welcome touch of light relief came to the station during the morning with the arrival of Detective Constable Peter Collier, with whom I would normally have shared Sunday duty. Peter was a shortish man who invariably wore his snap-brim trilby at the most rakish of angles while regarding the world with the humorous eye of the true East Ender. I recognised the jaunty footsteps and the cheery whistling as he came down the corridor. Clearly no one had warned him that the incident room was full of top brass. But once inside the door, he stopped dead in his tracks and his face was a study. He did the kind of double-take that you associate with the Laurel and Hardy films; and then as ever his native wit came to his aid. He looked slowly around the room. 'It's very kind of you all to give up your Sunday,' he said calmly, 'just to help me out with the crime book entries.'

The place erupted and no one was more amused than John Bliss, a commander who never lost the common touch.

Even without the statements of Bending and Simons, I am sure our enquiries would have led us to the Pen Club, for everything was beginning to fall neatly into place. The reappearance of a blood-stained Jeremiah Callaghan in Duval Street, the wounding of Billy Ambrose and the visit of Fay Sadler to the London Hospital had this one common link.

Fay Sadler was picked up at the home of Patrick Callaghan and brought in for questioning. She gave us a statement that largely echoed the points made earlier by Bending and Simons. She was, I suppose, the proverbial gangster's moll. Her long line of lovers had mostly come to strange and sticky endings. Tommy Smithson, one of her paramours, had been shot dead by hired killers in 1956. Two others had been murdered, while the rest had been wounded or badly beaten. She was a blonde lady of many secrets, very preoccupied and very hard. Yet despite her hardness, she was clearly nervous; and I sensed something of her dilemma. Her sympathies lay with the dead man and yet giving assistance to the police went against her whole way of life.

After she had left, I said to Roly Millington that I felt it unlikely she would ever tell her story in a witness box and he nodded soberly. 'You could well be right,' he said.

The evidence began to flow. A search of the Pen Club unearthed traces of blood, the spent cartridge case that Fay Sadler had tried to hide and a button stamped with the word 'FRENCH' and obviously torn from an article of clothing.

The cartridge case had almost certainly been ejected from the murder weapon which, according to our forensic experts, was a Beretta 6.3mm automatic pistol.

A search of Jimmy Nash's deserted flat in Charing Cross Road found a mac speckled with bloodstains that matched the blood group of Cooney. All the buttons were stamped with the word 'FRENCH' and one was missing. Forensic tests would prove that the button found in the Pen Club had been ripped from the mac of Jimmy Nash.

Doreen Masters was located at her Hampstead flat. At first she denied all knowledge of the Pen Club. But when asked to explain a blood-stained towel in her bathroom and further bloodstains on the passenger seat of her car (blood from the injured Johnny Read), she changed her story and was taken to Commercial Street for further questioning.

Read and Pyle were also brought in and positively identified by both Fay Sadler and Joan Bending. Simons failed to pick out either man. Later however, he admitted that he had recognised them both, but had been too frightened to say so. Coming events would show that he had good cause to be frightened.

Read had been arrested on his twenty-eighth birthday and I found him genuinely remorseful, a man out of his depth. He told me, 'This was just supposed to be a spanking. There weren't supposed to be any guns.' I believed him. He had a good record in the ring and had twice fought Dick Tiger. But like so many ex-boxers, he had been used by gangsters simply as a muscle man. He was the son of a policeman, a station sergeant at Streatham, a nice man and, as a result of this case, a broken man.

Joe Pyle was something else. Caught up in the twilight world of the gangster, he was slow to grasp the reality of his situation, namely, that a capital murder charge was hanging over him. But a spell in the cells of a police station, particularly one as grimly Victorian as Commercial Street, can have a sobering effect upon the hardiest of souls. A few hours after their arrest, Read and Pyle were overheard when talking through the grilles of their adjoining cells.

This is the gist from what I can remember of the officer's record of a very revealing conversation:

Read: I reckon Jimmy's done a bunk.

Pyle: Yes, I guess so.

Read: They all know who done it, you know. Don't make a statement saying you know the Nashes.

Pyle: I told them I know Ronnie.

Read: I think they know I know them. If we can get out, we might be able to get in touch with Jimmy.

Pyle: We will have to get a good brief (underworld slang for lawyer).

Read: My old man will have to fork out some money. We'll do a bit of porridge (prison sentence), you know. I suppose Ginger is running about doing something for us.

Pyle: They can't say we were concerned in the murder, can they?

Read: No, we never done any shooting. Three or four tried to get going into Nash. I said, 'Turn it up, boys.' It was a ruck (fight). And that was that.

Pyle: It's horrible, because they do not know what they are going to do you for.

Read: No. It's worrying.

Pyle: I'll lead a quiet life after this.

Read: Yes. All that gun business is silly, isn't it? I mean, they were only having a ruck to start with. When we get charged, that will be at a smaller court, won't it?

Pyle: It all depends what they charge us with.

Later, the dialogue continued.

Read: When that bloke Bliss spoke to me I told him I didn't know about the shooting.

Pyle: I won't go into any more clubs.

Read: Nor will I, Joe. I was thinking last night that they topped the three of us. If they topped me, my wife would be happy.

28

Pyle: Don't think that.

Read: Fay picked me out straight away, you know, and that other girl.

Pyle: Yes, me as well. But the bloke didn't, though.

Read: No. nor me.

Meanwhile the hunt for Jimmy Nash continued. He had kept away from all his known haunts and eventually it was the Nash family itself who made contact with us. They did so through their legal adviser, a certain Emanuel Fryde, a solicitor's managing clerk. He came to see Roly Millington by appointment and explained that he had been approached by William Nash, one of Jimmy's brothers, to act in this matter.

He said that Jimmy Nash had 'gone underground' and 'wouldn't be found in a million years.' The family were prepared to persuade Jimmy Nash to surrender only on condition that we (the police) did not make it a 'topping job,' meaning, of course, the possibility of an execution for the crime. Fryde said he fully appreciated that such an assurance couldn't be given and had explained this to William Nash. However, he was prepared to use his good offices to prevail upon the Nashes to produce Jimmy Nash, provided he received an assurance from Roly Millington that no pressure would be put upon the accused to make a statement, written or otherwise.

The assurance was given willingly and two days later Jimmy Nash arrived at City Road Police Station. He was accompanied by Emanuel Fryde who told Roly Millington, 'I understand you wish to see this man, James Lawrence Nash, in connection with a shooting affair last Sunday morning at Stepney when a man was shot dead. I want you to understand that he denies the charge of any kind at all. He is not guilty and acting on legal advice given to him, he is not making any verbal or written statement.'

Nash was brought to Commercial Street and I have seldom seen a man who appeared more devoid of human emotion. He was powerfully built with short-cut hair; and like Read and Pyle, he was an ex-boxer (although never in their league). He had a very quiet voice for such a violent man, but I don't recall him saying anything that seemed worth remembering.

He was a man of negative virtues – a non-smoker, non-drinker, who ate a pound of boiled sweets every day. He would sit in his cell, chewing them endlessly. Judging by the expression on his face, he could have been on another planet.

We charged Joe Pyle, Johnny Read, Doreen Masters and Jimmy Nash with the capital murder of Selwyn Cooney. But there was no great elation at Commercial Street. We knew that, for us, the real battle was only just beginning.

CHAPTER FOUR

CODE OF THE UNDERWORLD

'I am being faithful to the code by which I have lived.' Fay Sadler, explaining why she had remained in hiding from the police.

Shortly after the murder of Selwyn Cooney, a band of men armed with razors attacked Johnny Simons in a Paddington cafe. They slashed his face and left him lying there in a pool of blood. It was a tactical move that misfired.

After having made his initial statement, Simons had left his known address and gone into hiding. We had good reason to believe that we had lost a key prosecution witness. Certainly he was a man torn between divided loyalties. There was his loyalty to his murdered friend and there was also his instinctive obedience to the criminal's eleventh commandment: 'Thou shalt not grass' (the twelfth being 'Especially to the police'). The attack in that Paddington cafe was naturally designed to discourage him finally from taking the witness stand. Ironically it had precisely the opposite effect. Simons was, if you like, a small-time crook who liked to give the impression that he was more important in the criminal hierarchy than he really was, a bit of a braggart and definitely no angel. But he did have his pride and he could be game when it mattered.

That pride had been offended not so much because he had been slashed, but because he had been slashed in a public place in front of women and children. It needed twenty-seven stitches to put his face back together again. He remained in hiding until his wounds had healed and then he returned to his home address. This time he was quite determined to give his evidence and nothing was going to stop him.

The intimidation of witnesses had become so serious that we offered to place a continuous guard upon them. The offer was initially refused by them all. Fay Sadler and Joan Bending decided to lodge with Margaret Neill, the common-law wife of Cooney. They said they felt perfectly safe under this arrangement and Fay Sadler added, 'This will keep us away from the continual harassment of the press.' Joan Bending continued to work behind the bar at the New Cabinet Club where she presumably felt secure under the protection of Billy Hill. Even so, we kept a close watch over them and at least once a day, one of our officers would visit the club to make sure all was well.

The witness who would have strengthened the prosecution case immeasurably was Bill Ambrose. But after spending a month in hospital recovering from his wound, he insisted upon looking back at the incident with a Nelson-like eye. Although shot from the front at almost point-blank range, he was unable to identify the man with the gun, or for that matter, any of the men involved in the assault upon Cooney.

Now with some witnesses, this lapse of memory might have been put down to a fear of the consequences. But I don't believe that Ambrose was physically afraid of any man alive. He'd built a reputation in the ring as a tough and courageous fighter; and in this respect, he hadn't

31

changed. He didn't hesitate to respond to his wife's call, 'He's got a gun.' Even after having been shot, he still helped to carry Cooney down the stairs and into the street. Then, quite incredibly I think, he had gone home, looked at the wound which was a very serious one indeed, and then driven himself to hospital. No, I don't believe it was fear that held him back; just that code of silence adopted by the criminal fraternity.

While he was in hospital, I performed a couple of small favours for his wife – the kind of things any man would be happy enough to do for a woman whose husband was in intensive care. But on the day he came out, he made a point of thanking me. He wasn't effusive about it. That wasn't his style. He simply said, 'Thank you.' But many years later, he repaid that favour in his own way.

After I had been promoted to Commander and was enquiring into corruption offences I received a message saying that he had urgent information for me and wished to see me privately. This puzzled me initially; for giving information to police officers was most definitely not Billy Ambrose's style. But when we met, he told me that he had been invited to take part in a plot to discredit me.

He said that while on remand in Brixton Prison, he had been approached by someone he refused to name who had said: 'You know Bert Wickstead. He is causing a lot of trouble. He is rocking the boat. If you are willing to fit him up, saying you have given him money in the past, you will be given times and dates when it was available. You will have all the help, you could have the moon if you do it.'

He had turned down the offer. And to me, he said, 'I'm marking your cards. You've got to be careful.'

I had little doubt that he was telling the truth. He had nothing to gain by approaching me in this way. I had another good reason for taking the story seriously. There was always an element of corruption with any gangland enquiry, and the police officers involved who have much to gain in seeing me discredited. Those who were exposed were either proceeded against or they resigned the force. Allegations such as those that Ambrose had been asked to make are often hard to disprove. At the very least they would have caused me embarrassment and hampered my own investigation. But fortunately they picked the wrong man in Billy Ambrose. He had been a violent criminal with a way of life I would never attempt to defend. Nevertheless he had his own sense of fair play. And like the majority of professional villains, he had as little respect for bent coppers as I have. Which, just for the record, is none at all. Villains may use them from time to time, but they don't like them — and most definitely they can never trust them.

In the code of Billy Ambrose, it was *all right* to bear witness against police officers who wished to discredit another officer who was simply doing his job. But it was *wrong* to bear witness against the man who had shot him and come close to killing him. Just to make sure he couldn't be put in that position, he went to ground.

On the morning of 20 February, Margaret Neill rang to tell us that Fay Sadler had left her flat without warning during the night. We immediately launched a search to cover the city. All her known associates were visited, including Henry Callaghan — yet another member of the notorious family who described himself as 'originator and secretary of the Civil Liberties Association for the protection and defence of undesirables falling into police hands.' He had been quoted in the *Empire News* as claiming that he could produce Fay Sadler at any time, provided that the fee was adequate. When we asked him about this, he denied it hastily. We did trace Fay Sadler's current paramour, Roy Vernon Morgan, to an address in Catford. He admitted that he had been living with her since the disappearance, but didn't dare disclose her whereabouts. It was, he said, more than his life was worth. But it is perhaps significant that when traced he was in the company of Jeremiah and Patrick Callaghan. Despite the most strenuous efforts, we failed to find her before the trial. She surfaced again, albeit briefly, on the twelfth of May, and was interviewed by *Daily Express* reporter Victor Davis. In response to a phone call, he had met a man who only gave his name as 'Ted' at Cleopatra's Needle on the Embankment. 'Ted' offered to let him meet Fay Sadler and take photographs in return for a certain three-figure sum of money. The meeting was arranged to take place later that evening at the Anchor Public House in Clink Street, Southwark. Davis had given his word that police would not be told. He kept the appointment with a photographer and eventually Fay Sadler and 'Ted' walked into the bar.

'Ted' immediately demanded the agreed sum which was paid and the interview began. Later Davis would ask her whether she was satisfied with the arrangement of handing the fee to 'Ted' and she replied, 'Oh yes, he's a nice man. He's been minding me.' He asked her why she had disappeared and she said, 'I am being faithful to the code by which I have lived.' Before leaving, she told Davis, 'If you want to have a happy recollection of our meeting, you had better not leave this pub for ten minutes after I and my friends have gone.'

Several minor witnesses had gone to ground, clearly too scared to talk. This bid by the underworld to pervert the course of justice had begun to make many good police officers very angry. None more so than John Summerlin, a station sergeant at Commercial Street. One day, a well-known East End gangster with a reputation for mindless violence came marching into the station as though he owned the place. John slid out his truncheon from the shelf beneath the counter and brought it down with a crack across the top of the counter. 'If you have a lawful reason for being here, state it,' he said. 'Otherwise get the hell out of my station.' I happened to glance away for a moment and by the time I looked back, the man had gone. It was as though he had vanished into thin air. We never did discover why he'd come to see us. I suppose in this day and age that would have constituted grounds for a serious complaint against the police.

Meanwhile Joan Bending had quarrelled with Margaret

Neill, to no one's great surprise. They had, after all, been the mistress and common-law wife of Selwyn Cooney. a difficult relationship at the best of times.

Now, with threats growing, both Bending and Simons were anxious to accept our original offer of protection. We placed them in hotels just outside London. Eight police officers were detailed to guard them on a twenty-four-hours-a-day basis. And to make them even more secure, we changed hotels frequently. I had the very pleasant duty of making what we termed 'the money run'. This entailed visiting the hotels at least once a week, making sure that everything was moving smoothly and paying out the necessary living expenses to witnesses and policemen alike. The great boon in all this was that it gave me the chance to take my wife and small son on a run into the country. They provided the perfect cover.

Although they were as safe as they could ever hope to be, the outside pressures on our two witnesses continued to mount. Johnny Simons' girl friend, a twenty-three year old model called Barbara Ibbotson, was snatched in broad daylight from a Soho street and thrown into the back of a car. She was pinned to the floor while her attackers, taking their time, evidently enjoying their work, slashed her face four times. Three weeks later, she was slashed again. This time, twenty-six stitches were needed to staunch the flow of blood.

Joan Bending's pressures were even closer. We booked Joan Bending into an Elstree hotel which already had the actress Sophia Loren on its guest list. By some ill chance, the actress's jewels were stolen on our very first night. All very embarrassing and I wasn't about to win any popularity awards with either the hotel management or the local police who hadn't been told that we were there. Everyone seemed to jump to the conclusion that Joan had spotted the jewels and tipped off one of her criminal friends. Fortunately this wasn't so. Many years later, I interviewed the man who had stolen the jewels. He was a cat burglar who seemed to make a speciality of robbing

35

visiting actresses. He told us about an American film star with a spectacular style of love making. He was so intrigued that he returned to her house on five successive nights – just to watch!

In the space of a few brief weeks, Joan Bending had changed visibly. It was hard to recognise her as the girl who had screamed, 'You are all bastards.' Much of the credit for this change was due to the police officers detailed specifically to protect her, WPC Hilda Coles and Detective Constable Jim Singleton. Singleton was a big man with a pleasant easy-going sense of humour, but above all else a very decent human being. They had become friends. And I believe that for the first time in her life, Joan had come to realise that at least some policemen can be trusted. This was part of Roly Millington's wisdom. He had chosen the right officers for the job. It was a lesson I learned well. Gaining the trust of potentially hostile witnesses as well as the public is an essential facet of police work. And it's equally important that we should be worthy of that trust. Promises have to be kept at all costs. That was part of the creed I would preach to my own squads in the years ahead.

CHAPTER FIVE

GATHERING OF THE CLANS

'My son's death won't go unavenged.' Outburst from the father of Selwyn Keith Cooney at the conclusion of the trial.

The public gallery at the Old Bailey had the look of a gangsters' convention. The upper echelon of the underworld had come in force to see the trial of James Lawrence Nash. The Callaghans, interested bystanders from the start of the case, were there. So too were the Kray twins. I spotted many of the leading lights in the Billy Hill gang. And the Nash family had arrived in force. One might have imagined that their sympathies would have been sharply divided. Jimmy Nash, after all, stood charged with the capital murder of Selwyn Keith Cooney, a front man for Billy Hill, very much a rival concern. However, there was no open animosity. Nothing showed on their faces and the kind of emotions bubbling beneath the surface were anybody's guess. They spent a lot of time parading up and down on the pavement outside the court – and were especially prominent when witnesses were arriving or leaving. There was no doubt at all that the purpose of this was intimidation. On the first occasion that Joan Bending and Johnny Simons emerged, several of the mob surged forward in a threatening manner, and police officers had to intervene hastily.

On numerous other occasions, the City police had to clear the pavement. However, although these gangsters were in a mood bordering on anarchy, they still recognised resolute police action. And this, I think, is something worth remembering and pondering upon in view of today's climate of violence.

One point that interested me was the power structure within the Nash family. John 'Peacemaker' Nash, if you recall, had made that grandiose claim, 'I am the boss of the underworld.' But one only had to look to realise that he wasn't even boss in his own family. William 'Billy' Nash was clearly the major force in the clan, the titular head. Even the Krays listened to him with a certain respect.

The trial opened on 21 April 1960, and Nash shared the dock with Johnny Read and Joey Pyle. The charges against Doreen Masters had already been dismissed.

We now encountered two incidents of the kind which cause many police officers to worry deeply about the entire jury system. Firstly, one of the jurors when leaving the court looked towards William Nash and appeared to give a nod of recognition. We promptly investigated his background and discovered that he had been found guilty of theft as a juvenile. Furthermore, he was related by marriage to a family of violent East End criminals. While all this had been going on, one of the Nash fraternity was overheard to say, 'Well, never mind, we'll get one of the jury nobbled, and that will do it.' The man who picked up that whispered remark wasn't too sure about the tense. In other words, it could have been, 'We have got one of the jury nobbled.'

Because of the suspicious circumstances, the juror was kept under permanent observation by Flying Squad officers. As he left the court the following day, he was followed by officers in a nondescript vehicle. As the juror was about to drive away, a youth was seen to run from beside the driver's door of the car and join a man who had previously been standing alongside the Kray twins. The juror realised very quickly that he was being followed (a fact suspicious in itself) and attempted to take evasive action. When this failed, he stopped his car and challenged the officers.

The ensuing conversation is significant. First of all the juror said, 'Why are you following me about?'

When the officers didn't reply, he said, 'Are you police officers?' He was told they were and repeated, 'Why are you following me?'

The juror then made the most remarkable statement. 'I know what it's about. You won't catch me putting a foot wrong *now*.' The accent was heavily on the word 'now'.

Meanwhile a woman juror had visited her husband in Brixton Prison where Nash, Pyle and Read were being held on remand. Her husband then allegedly told the three men that his wife was on the Pen Club murder trial and had already made up her mind that Nash was guilty of capital murder. He had then given them his wife's home address.

All these facts were laid by the various counsel engaged before the judge, Mr Justice Gorman, in his room. He immediately discharged the jury and ordered a retrial.

Just before this had happened and while the jury were still in the box awaiting the arrival of the judge, we had yet another strange incident. That morning's *Daily*

Express carried a front page banner headline: 'MURDER JURY WATCH. YARD MAY PUT EXTRA GUARDS ON DUTY.' One of the Nash fraternity was seen to make a signal to our suspect male juror and then hold up that page so that he could see the headlines.

The trial that followed was notable for the fierce, one might almost say savage, attacks upon the characters of our two main witnesses, Bending and Simons. It has always seemed to me a strange facet of the law that defence counsel should be free to expose the criminal record and criminal connections of a witness. For remember, juries are never allowed to hear about defendants' previous convictions – though I have no doubt that time and again this truth would tip the balance and remove an evil man from society.

However, both Bending and Simons remained steadfast under cross-examination and couldn't be shaken in their story that Nash had fired the fatal shot.

In my opinion, the key moment in the trial came with Mr Victor Durand's address to the jury which surpassed anything I had ever heard before or since. It was brilliant, spellbinding stuff.

Although we were usually on opposite sides of the fence, I always had the greatest respect for Victor Durand. He was the old-style advocate with a wonderful command of the English language. Although he could be bruising in cross-examination, there was never anything personal about it. He was simply doing the job he'd been paid to do; and doing it as best he knew how. Which, in his case, was very well indeed.

The expression of Jimmy Nash barely changed throughout the entire trial. When the jury brought in a verdict of not guilty to murder, there wasn't a flicker of expression. No relief. No joy. Nothing.

When found guilty of grievous bodily harm and sentenced to five years, he seemed almost disinterested.

When Cooney's father, outraged by what he regarded as a terrible injustice, cried out, 'My son's death won't go unavenged,' Nash did turn his head slowly and gave the mere hint of a shrug, but the face still hadn't changed. He just seemed to be a man devoid of any true human emotion.

A police officer summed up the views of many of his colleagues when he said in a loud aside, 'What, grievous bodily harm on a dead man?'

I listened to the judge, Mr Justice Diplock, tell the jury, 'I have no doubt you have been shocked to learn the sort of thing that is going on in this city. Perhaps the most shocking thing of all is that some of these witnesses were scared — scared to tell the truth. It is a perfectly shocking thing.'

A few days later, we received an anonymous letter which doubtless summed up the views of one section of the underworld.

It said that they had decided to take the law into their own hands and carry out their own sentence of death on Jimmy Nash. They threatened that he would never know a moment's peace for the rest of his days, that he would be forever looking over his shoulder, and that they would get him in the end. It ended with the statement that enemies of the Nash family were 'tooling up' to decide who were the governors of London. Doubtless a response to that earlier vainglorious claim by Johnny Nash.

Subsequently I heard that Jimmy Nash was twice attacked in prison and beaten severely, losing half an ear on one of those occasions.

The Pen Club case probably ended any hopes that the Nashes might have had of gangland domination. They had transgressed the code of the underworld, which, even in cases of gang warfare, has never endorsed the 'permanent lesson'.

As promised, Johnny Simons was given a new identity and the chance of a new life in Spain. But he was soon hungering for the bright lights of home. He returned to England and was again slashed badly about the face. However I have good reason to believe that this had nothing at all to do with the Pen Club case. It was just a private bit of bother.

Jim Singleton and I escorted Joan Bending to King's Cross. She would spend a few months in Leeds with Cooney's father. Police officers would guard her on the train. Jim had become fond of her, and so had I. Still a teenager, she had gone through hell: the death of a lover; gangland threats; a long cross-examination that would have broken many strong men. She had survived it all and somehow had become a better person because of it.

I shook her hand and told her that she would remain under police protection until we were quite sure that she was safe again. Jim kissed her cheek.

Now I may have been mistaken. She was, after all, a girl who had kept violent company, a girl with no love for policemen. Just the same, as she waved us goodbye, I could have sworn there were tears in her eyes.

CHAPTER SIX

STOKE NEWINGTON

'Mind the cloth' … the appeal of teenage gunman John Brian McElligott when being handcuffed.

The jailing of Jimmy Nash may have changed the balance of power in the underworld. But it did nothing to change the pattern of crime on the streets where I worked. I stayed in G Division for a while and was then posted to N Division, serving at Kentish Town and Caledonian Road. The two stations were less than a mile apart and no one could ever describe the surrounding area as elegant. The houses were mostly terraced look-alikes, coated with the grime of ages. The streets were rough, tough and often violent. It was a good place for a copper to learn his trade. Although not strictly speaking the East End, it was nevertheless a part of London which I understood and in which I felt at home. I was very conscious of the fact that for every villain, there were a hundred honest, decent, hard-working citizens who needed our help. And this for me is what police work has always been about: the protection of the innocent.

On 11 February 1963, I was promoted to first-class sergeant and transferred to Barnet on S Division – and there I really plunged into inactivity and despair. Barnet is a pleasantly civilised part of Hertfordshire, a country station surrounded by nice, law-abiding people. In other words at that time, not an ideal spot for a first-class sergeant anxious to make his mark upon the force. My duties were purely supervisory, my most strenuous job that of working out the duty rosters. Barely a week went by when I didn't find some excuse to pay a visit to Scotland Yard – and once there I would make a point of bumping into the chief inspector in charge of postings. 'Please, please rescue me from this fate worse than death,' became my continual plea. Finally he did just that. He moved me to Dalston, a busy North London station where there was always more than enough to do. As if we didn't have enough local villains to cope with, young blacks had just begun commuting up on the tube from Brixton and picking pockets in Ridley Road Market. Meanwhile Dalston's young blacks were returning the compliment, travelling down to Brixton to commit their villainy. It's an age-old tradition. You don't commit crimes against the person on your own patch; because if you do there's always the danger you may come face-to-face with your victim the following day. This applies particularly to what I would term the street criminal – the rapist, the mugger, the pickpocket, the bag-snatcher and so on.

But there was another band of tearaways working the streets, a white teenage gang, who were causing us greater concern. They were carrying guns and had already shown that they were prepared to use them. The matter came to a head when a sergeant in a Q car was shot at by one of the gang. It was clear that we had to move quickly before someone was killed. Detective Superintendent Jock Forbes (of Cannock Chase fame) gave me a team of six young CID aides with instructions to hunt them down. During the following few weeks, we existed on the minimum possible amount of sleep as we worked around the clock. We questioned bands of Mods and Rockers and asked them for the name of any youngsters in the area known to carry a gun. Time and again, we were given the name 'Killer,' although no one seemed to know his real name or whereabouts. We were eventually tipped off that one of the gang was working on a building site immediately opposite Dalston police station. So I cleared the site and brought in all the workmen. Drastic, I know. But when guns are being carried on the street by teenagers crazy enough to use them, you need to be drastic. The foreman came charging into the station, full of outraged fury. The situation was then explained to him very politely and he was invited to stay. As I pointed out, he couldn't do a lot back there on the site without any men. The move paid off. We found the young gang member we were looking for and he in turn gave us the names and addresses of the rest.

During the investigation, we had heard so much about the reign of terror inspired by this young man known as 'Killer' that we were curious to meet him. And after finally getting his true name, John Brian McElligott, we came face to face with him for the first time. Quite a surprise. He stood five feet four inches and weighed seven stones dripping wet. He was frail, pale-faced, seventeen and dressed in the then popular style of the Mods. When we put the handcuffs on him, he pleaded 'Mind the cloth.' We were told that he had a history of childhood illnesses and was timid until the day he bought a gun, a Beretta. That changed everything. Soon he had a gang under his command and a reputation. A six foot four inch minder became his constant companion and it was said he gained Dutch courage by taking Purple Hearts.

But the judge at his Old Bailey trial, Carl Aarvold, echoed my own thoughts when he said, 'There seems to have been a poison growth affecting the youth of

Hoxton ... the core being McElligott who spread infection with all he came in contact. The influence he wielded depended upon his willingness to carry a gun and use it. One of the symptoms of the disease he spread was the failure of other youths to recognise the craven coward that he actually was.'

McElligott was found guilty of wounding a Stoke Newington youth, of shooting at the sergeant in the Q car and of unlawfully possessing a gun. He was jailed for five years. Six other members of the gang were sentenced to lesser terms.

It was, if you like, the start of my career as a gangbuster. The London *Evening News* described me as a tough East End cop and my squad as 'The Magnificent Seven.' All a bit grandiose. But when you're a first-class sergeant anxious to catch the eye of the top brass, you don't quibble too much about descriptions such as that.

On 21 June 1965, I got my promotion to detective inspector and I did wonder rather wistfully whether I might return to Hampstead in this new role. During my days as a young PC, I had very much envied the lifestyle of the then detective inspector who had the time to play golf in the afternoons and then play snooker downstairs with the superintendent. I felt that kind of thing would suit me rather well. But no such luck. Instead I was moved half a mile north to Stoke Newington which had long been renowned for its murders. These became so numerous that on one occasion we had five in a single week. The superintendent took charge of two, his deputy took one, I took one and the other was handled by a junior sergeant. You have to realise that we had already moved into the age of the Permissive Society. Violent men no longer had to fear the condemned cell and the rope. And all of a sudden life had become terribly cheap.

With murder so commonplace, the cases fail to shock you after a while or even to leave much impression on the mind. But two I do remember well, albeit for different reasons.

Early one morning, a dead man was found lying in

44

City Road. He had been stabbed through the chest. Although it was outside our area, I was given the case because of my local knowledge. I went down there with Big Jim Singleton (Joan Bending's one-time bodyguard) and by three o'clock the same day it was all over. We had picked up our murderer, handed him over to the superintendent at City Road and written out our reports. A neat bit of detection, if I do say so myself, and one which I consider merited a commendation. But a very senior police officer thought otherwise – expressing the view that, 'Wickstead was only doing his job, after all.'

The other murder is remembered solely for its motive – or one might say lack of motive. This case too began with the discovery of a dead body in the road. It was 6.15 a.m. and broad daylight when I arrived on the scene with Superintendent Edward Howlett. The dead man had been stabbed in the stomach and was lying in a pool of blood. Superintendent Howlett searched his pockets, finding a bingo club membership card in the name of S. Sammon and a recorded delivery slip. These enabled us to identify him as Sean John Joseph Sammon, an Irishman who until recently had been living in Stoke Newington. We traced his friends and family and the story soon emerged. The previous evening, he had walked into a fish and chip shop and moved past the queue to talk to the proprietor whom he knew well. A Scot named Walker Harrington was standing at the front of the queue. He assumed that Sammon was jumping the queue, became very angry and told him to take his place at the back.

After a brief exchange of words, Sammon – described to us as a mild and even-tempered man – did indeed move to the back of the queue, and one might have imagined that this would be the end of the matter. But the anger stayed with Harrington and as he left the shop, witnesses heard him say that he was going home to get a knife. Some half an hour later, he encountered Sammon and his friends on the street and produced a knife which he waved in front of Sammon's face. Very shortly afterwards, the fatal blow was struck.

Harrington, a medium-sized man with a broad Scottish accent, was brought into the station. He had spent most of his days in the Gorbals area of Glasgow and was no stranger to violence. Six years earlier, he had stabbed another man, again in the stomach, and had been jailed for grievous bodily harm. He had only quite recently been released. He was nervous when interviewed and the first thing he said was, 'You can put away those papers, because I'm not making any statement.' However, he then proceeded to speak quite freely, claiming that he had only fetched the knife for the purpose of self-protection. Up until this point, he had kept his head down and spoken in little more than a mumble. But as he began to describe how he had produced the knife and brandished it in front of Sammon, his whole attitude changed. The hesitancy went away. He became confident, almost aggressive.

As he relived the moment, it was as though the knife was back in his hand. Shades of McElligott, I think. With McElligott, a gun had brought about the transformation. With Harrington, a knife had served the same purpose.

Harrington showed no signs of remorse. He was a hard little man, but I will give him credit for one thing. He was determined to shield his young wife. She had been involved in the affray before the stabbing took place. She had slapped the face of one of Sammon's friends and had then been forcibly restrained by her own brother. But when I asked Harrington whether she had been carrying any knives for him that night, he said flatly, 'You can leave her out of it. I have told you this is down to me.'

When we asked him where he'd left the knife used in the stabbing, he said it was in the kitchen of his home. And instantly I knew he was lying. It's one of those strange things. But when interviews become part of your daily life, you eventually come to a stage when instinct takes over and you can sort out the lies from the truth

46

beyond all possible doubt. And so it proved. The knives in Harrington's kitchen hadn't been used in the stabbing of Sammon. I then enlisted the help of the local council with their drain-sucking devices – and we eventually found a knife in a drain nearby.

Harrington's wife was very young and very frightened, but at the same time very loyal to her husband. There was clearly violence in her nature and yet she did at least show genuine regret. This was borne out by two witnesses who both heard a woman wailing in the darkness, 'Oh God, why did you do it?' A broad Scottish accent had replied, 'It was his fault. He started it.'

Still, as I was saying. I have remembered that murder for just one reason. A man walks into a fish and chip shop and is accused – incorrectly, as it turned out – of jumping the queue. And for that reason, he dies. It would be hard to think of a more trivial motive for murder.

Another example of just how cheap life had become was provided by a series of attacks carried out on a colony of Orthodox Jews who resided in the Stoke Newington area. You couldn't have hoped to find a more harmless, more law-abiding band of people. They would never raise a hand to anyone – or for that matter, even their voice. Yet the young trainee rabbis were being constantly stabbed and assaulted. Some of the stabbings were so severe that it's something of a miracle that none of them died. We were all too well aware of the fact that unless we put a stop to this very quickly someone would indeed die. So we sent out the troops, kept watch and protected them as best we could.

We eventually arrested a seventeen year-old who admitted that he had carried out some of the assaults as a kind of game, if you please, on these funny-looking people. That's what he called them: 'funny-looking people'. He belonged to a youth club and that's where we found most of the other teenagers who had taken part in the assaults. We arrested nine of them. Their ages ranged from fifteen to nineteen and they all came from good, decent, respectable families who'd had no idea that this had been happening. The parents, without exception, were totally shocked when they arrived at the police station and learnt of their son's involvement in this stabbing of the innocent. When the time came for the youngsters to be moved from the interview room to the charge room, the parents were shown out – and the boys were about to walk there at their own leisurely pace. But I had a sergeant named Paddy Cully who had other ideas about this. Paddy had served with a Dominion police force in Southern Africa, and had never lost his military manner. He carried a swagger stick and looked every inch the traditional sergeant-major. As such, he lined up the boys, tallest to the right, shortest to the left, and marched them to the charge room, barking out his orders along the way. It didn't cheer up the boys too much, but it seemed to please some of the parents who later told us that it was good to see their sons getting a touch of much-needed discipline.

I should add that Paddy, despite his eccentricities, was a first-class police officer. There was a night when Paddy and I were the only two in the station. He came into my office to say, 'Guv, there's a man outside. He says he thinks he's stabbed another man to death.'

'Well, has he, Paddy?' I asked. 'Has he really stabbed him to death?'

Paddy shook his head slowly. 'I don't know, Guv. If he has, he's very calm about it all.'

'Maybe you'd better bring him in,' I said.

A middle-aged, powerfully-built coloured man was then ushered in. I could see that his jaw was swollen and that he was bleeding from the left side of his mouth. But as Paddy had said, he did seem remarkably calm and collected, and it was this calmness which had thrown Paddy. The man explained in a quiet voice how he had quarrelled with another man in the kitchen of his house. The other man had struck him with a jug and in a flash of anger, he had picked up a knife and stuck it in him. In this man's case, I have no doubt that it was a flash of anger which would be regretted for a lifetime. For he didn't strike me as a violent man. Nor did I doubt his story for a moment.

I told Paddy, 'I think we have a murder on our hands.'

'Oh, my God,' said Paddy and somewhat to my surprise, left the office at a rate of knots.

I later learnt that he had then nipped into the pub which virtually adjoined the station, sunk a quick double Scotch and, equilibrum recovered, returned, brisk and ready for action. The story we'd been told proved true enough. The other man involved in the fight had been taken to the Prince of Wales Hospital and was dead on arrival. I then sent Detective Brendan Byrne (who would prove to be such a tower of strength in the years ahead) to the house where the stabbing had taken place. I told him to bring everyone in, but to make sure that the house remained untouched. I had reason to be glad that I had given those instructions. For when the forensic team arrived they were able to corroborate the story we'd been told almost word for word. There was the broken jug with the fingerprints of the dead man. Signs of a violent, but brief struggle. And in the dustbin – again just as our coloured friend had said – they found the knife. I never met a more cooperative prisoner on a murder charge – or one for whom I had more sympathy.

A few weeks later, we received a tip-off from one of our informers that a chemists' wholesalers was about to be robbed by a five-man team of top villains. We were given the day and the time on which the dummy run would take place. Normally a job such as this would have been handed over to the Flying Squad. But I had never been overfond of the Flying Squad and there was no way in which I was going to let them in on this one. We set up an observation point in the top room of a pub immediately opposite the warehouse and watched the dummy run through binoculars. Only two of the villains appeared at this stage and it was fascinating to watch them rehearse each part of the operation. Not for the first time, I wondered why men capable of planning with such skill and precision don't apply their minds to more honest ventures. I am convinced that many of the top villains could make fortunes in legitimate business. Having watched the dummy run, we knew exactly what to expect on the night – and this time we were the ones who timed our move to perfection. At a given signal, Q cars, dogs and a vanload of policemen arrived at the warehouse. It was all over in a matter of seconds. The villains were too shocked to offer any resistance. That night's work had saved £500,000 worth of goods and done the reputation of Stoke Newington nick no harm at all.

In fact, I was fortunate to have some very good men with me at the station. My first-class sergeant, for instance, was Geoff Chambers. Geoff is now a chief superintendent and was in charge of the Neilsen (House of Horrors) case. We had our fair share of characters too. There was a sergeant who shall be nameless, because he is now married and, I'm told, treading the path of virtue. But he used to be rather fond of a lunchtime drink. And if he was ever missing in the afternoon, we always knew where to find him, sound asleep in the hay in the Stables, beside his pet horse. Although it had its funny side, this clearly wasn't a practice to be encouraged. Nor was I over-happy at a situation that had existed long before I came to the station. Round about eight-thirty every evening, the officers on the nine a.m.-to-ten p.m. shift would adjourn with their informants, to the local pub (known in the station as The Annexe) for the last hour or so of their duty. It meant that if they were ever needed in a hurry, we could lose five vital minutes in rounding them up. I could, of course, have ended the practice with a direct order. But this would have caused resentment and damaged the sense of teamwork and loyalty which I had been carefully building up. So I decided to be a bit more subtle than that. I started a card school to cover that last hour of duty. Some still preferred to slip off to the pub with the understanding that they stayed near a phone for instant recall. But I nevertheless now had a solid nucleus of officers in the station ready to cope should any emergency arise.

One night when the school was still in its infancy, the superintendent walked in. He was filled with instant fury. 'How dare you play cards on duty?' he stormed and turning to me, he added, 'Inspector, I would like a word with you in my office.'

I followed him and was just about to receive a rucking when I said, 'Just a moment, sir, think on this ... ' And I proceeded to explain precisely why I had started the school. I had got halfway through my explanation when the balloon went up. We suddenly had a very serious multiple assault and GBH on our hands. And then there was really no need to say any more. The point had been made. We had the men ready to move that instant. Thereafter the school became a regular feature of our nights at Stoke Newington.

It is often asked in cases of murder and unnatural death, why is a post mortem necessary? Of course the logical answer is to determine the cause of death. It may be different from that which appears, and an incident at Stoke Newington brought this very vividly home to me.

I was called out one Sunday morning to a room on the top floor of a three-storey Victorian dwelling in the Manor House area. It was in a great state of disorder, the chairs and table overturned, smashed crockery on the floor, curtains torn from the windows, and lying on the bed was the body of a young woman aged about twenty-five.

The bedclothes were balled up under her, the pillow was on the floor, and she was naked. Clearly visible was the large number of bruises upon her body, face, arms and legs. Both eyes were blacked and she had been bleeding from the mouth and nose. The inescapable impression to a police officer was that she had been beaten to death, and this in fact was why I had been called. The divisional surgeon had made a preliminary

51

examination of the body and in his opinion death had occurred sometime between ten and eleven p.m. the previous evening.

Enquiries were made in the house and it was ascertained that the girl had a boy friend who visited her regularly and the two were often heard by the other tenants to quarrel violently. One such quarrel had indeed occurred the previous evening. A search of the dead woman's handbag revealed the name and address of the boy friend, and at that stage I must confess I thought that he had committed murder. Leaving instuctions for photographs and forensic examinations and for the body to be removed to the mortuary, I went and arrested the boy friend and returned to Stoke Newington police station with him.

He freely dmitted that he had been the dead woman's boy friend for about eight months and that they frequently quarrelled. There had been one such quarrel the previous night and he had struck her once in the face to stop her screaming. He thought he had blacked her eye. Had she complained about his behaviour? He went absolutely rigid with shock when I told her she was dead and was most vehement in his denials that he had killed her, swearing that he had only hit her once.

I had him placed in a cell and then went to the mortuary. The pathologist was Professor Francis Camps, Bernard Spilsbury's worthy successor and with Keith Simpson, and Donald Teare, one of the foremost forensic pathologists in the world. I told him about the police investigation so far, about the boy friend, and his statement that he had only struck the woman once. He thanked me and agreed that part of the bruising on the face was consistent with a blow from a fist, but he wasn't certain about all the rest.

His post mortem was very carefully and painstakingly done, and at the conclusion he said, 'Sorry, you'll have to let the boy friend go, he didn't kill her.' Once I had digested this, he went on to explain and reconstruct the 'crime'. The woman was epileptic and after the boy friend had left her the previous night she had a more than usually violent fit and all the bruises (apart from boy friend's black eye) had been caused by her throwing herself about during this fit. The damage in the room had been caused by it, the bleeding from the mouth was from her bitten tongue, before she had swallowed it and on one of her legs was imprinted the pattern of the beading on top of the skirting board of the room.

As a postscript to this little tale, when I made enquiries about these fits from her boy friend, family and other friends, everyone professed ignorance of her medical problem. We were never able to ascertain whether or not she had been treated for her complaint and if in fact she knew herself. Would it have saved her life had she known of it and been treated? Of one thing I am sure, the most relieved man in the world that day was the boy friend when he was released. It also made me ponder the point that if this had happened before the days of pathologists, would he have been charged with murder, and indeed would he have hanged?

CHAPTER SEVEN

THE QUEEN OF THE NAZIS

'Jews are our misfortune.' Françoise Jordan

Françoise Jordan walked into the most famous court in the world, Number One at the Old Bailey. She was dressed in black, the colour of the Gestapo. Black leather coat. Black leather kneeboots. A gold swastika dangled from a chain around her neck. Another swastika was worn on her arm. A buzz swept the crowded courtroom followed by a stunned silence.

It was Mr Justice Phillimore who broke the spell. 'Madam,' he said, 'remove that symbol from your arm. You will not turn this court into a political arena.'

She started to protest and the judge's face turned to

stone. 'Madam,' he repeated, 'remove that symbol.' After a moment's hesitation, she obeyed, wise enough to recognise the authority of an English judge in an English court of law.

She was appearing as a defence witness in a case which had become known as 'The Synagogue Burnings'. Following that case, I was commended on behalf of my squad. As a result of our work, a particularly unpleasant brand of racism had been checked, ten arsonists had been given prison sentences and the Jewish community of North London would sleep more peacefully in their beds.

But mixed with the satisfaction over a job well done, there was a sense of frustration. I didn't believe that justice as yet had been fully done inasmuch as Françoise Jordan was still at liberty. The defendants had deserved their sentences. And yet they were really little more than young pawns in the game – bewitched by the most fanatically dangerous woman I have ever met. The press called her 'The Queen of Britain's Nazis'. But she would have been more aptly described as the prophetess of a master race. Very beautiful, very eloquent and very evil.

Her flaxen hair gave her a Germanic look and yet she had been born in France. She was the niece of Christian Dior, the French couturier – and was only three years old when the Germans invaded her homeland. She had stood in the garden, waving a German flag, watching the tanks roll by. She was fond of saying that this was the moment which changed her life. After marrying a count, her full name became Marie Françoise Suzanne, la Comptesse de Caumont La Force. But the marriage was short-lived and thereafter her choice of men appeared to be governed by their political persuasions. She was engaged to John Hutchyns Tyndall, the leader of the Greater Britain Movement; and then married Colin Jordan, the leader of the rival Fascist organisation, the British National Socialist Party. This marriage went the way of the first. She described Jordan as a weak man, meaning that his policies weren't as forceful as she would have wished.

I had been steadily building up evidence against her

and was almost ready to make my move when she fled the country, and took refuge in France. It was frustrating, but I had the feeling she would return. Her leading disciples were still in London and political power was her guiding star.

The synagogue burnings began in the spring of 1965 and by the time the year had run its course, no less than thirteen London synagogues had been set on fire. During this period, I was a detective inspector at Stoke Newington, an area noted for its large Jewish population. Their main synagogue was called the Sha'are Shomayim and it incorporated a Jewish boys' school. On the night of 31 July, the back of the synagogue was set on fire by a petrol device. Fortunately the flames were spotted quickly and put out before too much damage was done.

Some anti-Semitic words had been daubed on the wall in spray-on paint: 'Heil Hitler'; 'Werewolf'; and 'We shall free Britain from Jewish rule'. But by the time I arrived the following morning, they had been erased on the orders of the rabbi. He didn't want either the boys or his congregation to see them.

Detective Jim Singleton was with me. Naturally we wanted to enter the synagogue. However, the rabbi was adamant. First, we had to wear hats. The fact that I was a police officer, trying to investigate a crime, was seemingly irrelevant. No one, but no one, we were told, walked bare-headed in a synagogue.

After a hasty turning out of cupboards, I was given one of those little Jewish caps and Big Jim who is well over six feet and nearly as wide, was handed one of the rabbi's spare top hats. I was grateful that there were no photographers in sight as we moved down the aisle. A more odd looking couple of policemen you've never seen.

I gathered up all the forensic exhibits and had them retained against the day when I hoped we would apprehend the arsonists. We were naturally making enquiries about extreme right-wing organisations such as the National Socialist Movement. And in the end, we had the kind of lucky break that you need on most investigations. A young man was arrested following a Fascist meeting in Dalston, and subsequently fined for possessing an offensive weapon. He was a card-carrying member of the NSM. In fact, he was about to be promoted to the rank of lieutenant-colonel in the British SS. But he also had several Jewish friends. In particular, he had a Jewish girl friend whom he was anxious to impress. All of which may help to explain why he had a sudden change of heart. He volunteered to make a full confession and admitted that he had been involved in the burning of the Sha'are Shomayim synagogue. He also named his confederates and explained how they had set fire to this synagogue and placed incendiary devices in others. As a result of this, several people came to see me at my invitation. They included Malcolm Robert Sparks and Hugh Llewellyn Hughes.

Sparks admitted he was the group leader with the rank of lieutenant-colonel. But he said he preferred his rank in 'civilised' German. His rank was *Obersturmbannfuhrer*. He was, incidentally, just nineteen. He stated that the leader of the movement was Colin Jordan, adding, 'a true Englishman'. He was wearing a black swastika badge in his lapel and admitted proudly that it was the insignia of the Dutch Waffen SS.

A few days later, I went with Detective Brendan Byrne to Sparks' home. After searching the place, we took him back to Stoke Newington station. It was raining and our car narrowly avoided a collision with a taxi which had skidded. I said to Brendan, 'If he'd hit us and we'd been in a Mini, we wouldn't have had much chance.'

Before he could reply, Sparks said, 'Well, if you had a Panzer, you could drive through all these Jewish houses and see the colour of their wallpaper.' I repeat: he was nineteen years old.

Back at the station, I told him that two of his friends had been arrested, and that they'd both made statements. He raised his hands in surrender and shouted, *'Alles kaput.'*

The first two could have been described as little more than foolish boys. But Hughes was a different proposition, a hard man known as the 'Mad Bomber' amongst his associates. He had served in the Welsh Guards and it may not have been entirely coincidental that some of the detonators used to set off the fire bombs were of a military pattern. He said he didn't think I had any evidence to connect him with the fires 'apart from what a bunch of weak-willed fools have told you'. He was then shown all the forensic evidence, a brace and bit, a green nozzle and plastic that had been collected at the time of the fire. He then asked to see other evidence and then with a fine piece of bombast said, 'There isn't any more, is there? It was destroyed in the fire, wasn't it? And if it wasn't, I shan't tell you anything about it.'

I warned him that he was about to be charged and he told me that I was making the greatest mistake of my life. Then, as if he had relinquished his British heritage, he said, 'Your British justice will let me out.'

He was later taken to the North London Court where he came face to face with Malcolm Sparks, who said, 'Hello, Hugh, long time no see. They got Paul and that's how it all started.'

Hughes replied, 'Yes, I know. It's a pity he couldn't keep his mouth shut. If he had, we wouldn't be here now.'

On 15 February 1966, at the Old Bailey, Hughes was found guilty and sentenced to five years imprisonment. Sparks got four years.

During the investigation, we learned that there was some form of organised Jewish surveillance to shadow our movements. Whether this was to make sure I was doing the job properly, I'm not sure. But it was always there in the background. And after the trial, Brendan Byrne and I had reason to be grateful to this band of men whom we termed our 'League of Shadows'. We had come out of the Old Bailey and were crossing the road to our car when some of the Fascist supporters began to walk towards us. They were clearly intent on mischief. But before this could happen, a second circle of men appeared surrounding the Fascists and these were some of the biggest and most menacing-looking fellows I'd ever seen. If they weren't Jewish, they certainly had the right affiliations. They were converging, not on us, but on the Fascists. They, after having done a double take, realised that they could be in peril and there was no time lost, as they say in official circles, in 'evacuating the area'. And, I may add, with some degree of speed.

When the dust had settled, one of our shepherds – the smallest of the lot, about six feet two inches, with shoulders to match – came up and said in broken English, 'We are on your side. May we have some pictures for the newspapers in Israel?'

Having given our heartbeats time to return to something like normal, we posed happily enough for our new-found friends.

But the case was far from closed. Another group of arsonists, all members of the NSM, had to be caught and put away. The most bizarre young man in this group was John William Evans, known throughout the movement as 'The Undertaker'. Not only did he look like one, being lank and lugubrious, but he also insisted upon driving an old hearse around the streets. He admitted to setting fire, or attempting to set fire, to no less than seven Jewish synagogues. He chose to write his own statement of admission.

For the first time, we were being given evidence of Françoise Jordan's direct involvement. According to Evans, she had expressed a desire to take part in the burning of a synagogue at Stanmore. She had ridden in a car with Evans and his fellow conspiritors. But when they arrived, the synagogue lights were on. Considering the risk too great, they had abandoned the attempt.

It was during this part of the investigation that I again encountered my League of Shadows. I knew that a militant group of Jews had planted a spy in the ranks of the NSM. I badly wanted to meet him, and made this wish known through my Jewish connections. I received a cryptic phone-call telling me to be in my office at ten that night.

On the stroke of the hour, a black Mercedes drew up outside the front door of Stoke Newington station. Four of my Shadows from the Old Bailey got out with a little man in their midst. They walked into the station, picked the little man up and put him over the counter. One of them announced, 'Mr Wickstead wants him.' And then they were gone.

The little man proved to be very cooperative. He remained with me for most of the night, making a long and detailed statement. He made it quite clear that Françoise Jordan had been the instigator of the violence. This information coupled with the statements of Evans the Undertaker and one of his associates formed the basis of a strong case against her.

The Shadows offered to bring her to Britain with no questions asked. I couldn't restrain my curiosity. I said, 'Well, how do you propose to do that?'

Their spokesman shrugged. He said, 'Perhaps it's better that you don't know. All you have to do is be present in a field somewhere in the Home Counties one dark night and she will be delivered to you.'

Obviously, no police officer could be a party to that. Still, it was a delicious thought at the time. Shades of Eichmann. I think the DPP's representative thought so too. Was there a hint of a smile when I told him?

I had always been confident that Jordan would return eventually of her own free will, and sure enough she did. She slipped very quietly into the country and I was tipped off that she was staying with one of her more ardent disciples in Dagenham.

Detective Sergeant Colin Ashdown brought her by car to Stoke Newington. She walked into my office, perfectly groomed, calm, composed and seemingly very confident.

I began by asking her why she had fled to France. She gave this some thought, and then replied, 'I was not – how shall I say – scared of you. I went for personal reasons.'

As the interview went on, she would occasionally

glance around the room in a disinterested sort of way. And then her eyes would meet mine. It may have been imagination, but I think I detected a mocking look in them as though she was saying this was a game we were playing – a game that only she could win.

I said, 'It is a fact, is it not, that you hate the Jewish race?'

She nodded. 'Yes, I make no secret of this.'

'It is said that you have a liking for quoting Julius Streicher, one of Hitler's ministers; in particular his saying, "Jews are our misfortune." Is this true?'

She nodded again. 'I know this one, and lots of others. This one is true and also the others.'

In answer to another question, she said, 'Everybody talks about what they would like to do to the Jews, myself as well. The gas chambers were too humanitarian for them.'

As she talked about the Jews, the casual air went away and hate took over. Her words came faster and a strange look came into her eyes. It occurred to me that at times the dividing line between fanaticism and madness becomes very thin indeed.

Part of her confidence was based on what she clearly considered a cast-iron defence.

When I asked her whether she'd been responsible for the organisation and the planning of the synagogue burnings, she contrived to look very innocent.

'Responsible?' she said, 'I did not start the fires. If I say I want something done which should be done and it is done, I am not responsible if I am not there.'

With a touch of the born actress, she took the thought a stage further. 'Why should anyone do what I want done? I have English ways. I dream out loud.'

The jury, having heard all the evidence, thought otherwise. The judge, Mr Justice Cusack, sentenced her to eighteen months in jail.

She stood very straight and there wasn't a flicker of emotion on that beautiful face. True to her code, she

clicked her high heels together and shouted defiantly,
'Heil Hitler!'

CHAPTER EIGHT

BLUE MOVIE MURDER

'Gerry started growling like an animal.' Michael
John Muldoon.

It was one of those beautiful early days of summer that
make a man glad to be in England. I was driving through
the Essex countryside, thinking about my new and
challenging job. Only three days previously, I had been
promoted to detective chief superintendent and posted to
J Division, a huge area which includes Epping Forest.
This was the first time since then that I'd had a chance to
relax and enjoy the sunshine. But not for long. A
message was coming over the radio: 'The body of a man
has just been found in the forest.' Policemen get
hardened to tragedy and I must confess that my first
reaction was, 'Another bloody suicide.' Epping Forest
has for long been a favourite haunt for people wishing to
take their own lives.

I found the body in a ditch, fifty yards from the road
and close to a field which schoolchildren used as a nature
centre. It was that of a very powerfully built man. He
was face down and unclothed, except for a pair of black
bikini-style trunks. One look was enough to realise that
this was no suicide, but a particularly dreadful murder.
The victim had received no less than eighty-nine stab
wounds.

I sealed the area and started a detailed examination. An
officer made notes as I spoke aloud my findings. Twelve
feet from the body, and at right angles to it, were car tyre
tracks. Alongside the track nearest the body was a
bloodstained area of ground three feet by two feet, but
only surface-stained. Eight inches from this was a small

stone with a blood splash on it, and three feet from that was another small stone, similarly stained. The stones were at the most an inch in size, the bloodstains barely an eighth of an inch. Just specks. Plaster casts and photographs were taken of the tracks and the stones photographed and preserved.

The pathologist arrived, a woman, Dr Ivy Tuck. Two of my senior officers advised me to dispense with her services as she was virtually unknown, and to call in someone more renowned. But there was an air of calm commonsense about her that I liked. So I refused and have good reason to be glad that I did. Today the case has become a classic in the forensic field, and much of the credit for that belongs to Ivy, who became a great friend to myself and my family.

From her initial examination, she formed the opinion that the murder had taken place somewhere else, and that the body had simply been dumped. She also suspected that most of the blood had been drained or had leaked elsewhere. A later examination proved her right.

My first major problem was to identify the body. There were no marks or labels on the trunks, nothing on the body except tattoos. Indeed, the post-mortem examination established that the body had been cleaned.

We ran a fingerprint check, which came up with nothing. We published descriptions and photographs of the tattoos in the press. One tattoo pictured monkeys, another a lion's head, and there were theories that he might have belonged to a Far Eastern secret society. We asked Hong Kong to assist. Result: nothing. Seamen's hostels and shipping offices were canvassed. Again, nothing. We even asked the pathologist to work on his eyes, head and face, so that a presentable picture could be taken for circulation. But in the event, this was not necessary.

The fingerprint department at Scotland Yard ran a further check. And four days after the discovery of the body, Commander Bob Peat gave me the welcome news that the dead man had been identified as Gerald Patrick

Joseph Hawley, a criminal with no less than eleven convictions for violence. His associates included the notorious Kray twins. So we had the possibility of a gang-war murder. With that thought in mind, we examined the premises above the twins' Regency Club – and found nothing.

The file on Hawley also revealed West End pornographic connections, and because of this I directed that everyone named on that file should be seen. As a result of these enquiries, we discovered that Hawley had been living in a luxury flat at Bedford Hill, Balham, and by half-past nine that night I was there.

I have never seen any house, flat or living quarters as clean as this one. It positively glistened. From an all-night forensic and fingerprint examination, only one small well-dried blood spot on an otherwise clean towel was found. Tests later revealed it as the murderer's. There was not a single fingerprint belonging to Hawley. It was patently obvious that a lot of time had been spent on the cleaning exercise. But whatever the purpose might have been, I was confident that this hadn't been the scene of the murder. Violent death has a smell all its own. After you've seen more than your fair share of murder, you come to recognise it instinctively. Hawley hadn't died here. Of that, I was sure.

A note had been pinned to the front door, addressed to 'Mick' and asking him to phone Pauline and Margo. From the phone number, we got their address and interviewed them. We learned that the flat had been taken by Hawley and his partner 'Mick' under false names. Hawley had called himself Anthony Simpson and Mick had used the name Dennis Morden. Both had recently come out of prison, hence the use of aliases. The flat had been used by them as a studio to make blue films. The two girls had played some part in their production.

It transpired that the murderer and others had cleaned and polished the flat to remove all traces of the dead man and the blue film business. Unfortunately for them, the note was pinned on the door just fifteen minutes after they'd left the scene.

From the girls we got an address in Stockwell Road, Brixton, where they thought the mysterious Mick lived, and at about five o'clock in the morning, we arrived there. It was now nineteen hours since the identification of the body, and my team and I had been going non-stop.

We knocked and, receiving no answer, we entered the flat. The first thing that struck me was the smell of paint, which was very strong, but not strong enough to hide the underlying smell of death. I was already convinced, beyond all doubt, that this was where Hawley had died. Everything we found in those hours before the dawn served to confirm that impression. The stair carpet had been removed, but the under-felt strips were still there, plus a roll of new carpet. The skirting boards and stair ends were newly painted in green. The walls appeared to have been washed. But just above a light switch going up the stairs, we found a splash of blood. On a light socket in a passageway, we found more blood splashes. There were gaps in the banister rails of another flight of stairs. Remember, the pathologist had said the body had been drained of blood. We found it in that flat, most of it soaked into an expensive leather settee, the remainder under floorboards and behind skirting-boards. Blood is an extremely hard substance to remove or wash away. This flat proved the point. The murderer thought he had got rid of it. How wrong he was!

Looking at this flat, the missing banister rails, and the new carpet, I suddenly remembered something. I ran back down the stairs to an alley at the side of the house. There with the dustbins was a collection of rubbish, including the broken banister rails and an empty green paint tin. Plus a towel, bandages and a lamp shade – all bloodstained. Fate appeared to be working against the murderer. Firstly, there had been the note pinned to the door, and now this. On the morning after the murder, the dustmen were due to empty the bins. Instead, they had chosen to go on strike – thus leaving the rubbish there for our examination. And tests showed that most of the blood belonged to the same group as the victim's.

We established that the occupiers of the flat were Michael John Muldoon (the mysterious Mick) and his wife Sandra. In the other flat, served by the common entrance and stairway, lived Kenneth Charles Eighteen, the husband of Muldoon's sister. All three of these worthies were missing.

However, before we left the flat, there was a strange little episode. Following a discreet knock, we opened the door to confront a well-dressed young man with a small suitcase, asking for Muldoon and Eighteen. He was invited to open his case. The contents, the latest selection of blue films from the Continent. He was acting as a courier for the pornographic movie trade. He was horribly shocked to learn why we were there and, subsequently, was dealt with elsewhere.

The blue movie link in this case was looming larger all the while. From our enquiries, we learned that Muldoon had built up a considerable empire. He was said to be earning more than £2,000 a week and boasted that he had £150,000 in a numbered bank account in Switzerland. He imported films from Scandanavia and exported the films he made in Britain. He paid his models £10 per film and sold those films at £25 a copy. The profit was sometimes five hundred per cent. On top of this, there was the sale of pornographic 'stills'. When we visited the headquarters of his company, Climax Films, in Great Windmill Street, Soho, we found more than one hundred and twenty canisters of film. A considerable haul.

Hawley had starred (if that's the right word) in several of Muldoon's films. He had also worked for Muldoon as a blue-movie courier and bodyguard. We were told of an occasion when he beat up a man on the orders of Muldoon. Many of the people we spoke to talked about his strength. One had seen him tear the doors off a car with his bare hands. Another recalled the night when eight policemen had been required to overpower him. A girl told us how she had taunted him by saying, 'You're not a man. Anyone can hit a woman.' According to her, he then smashed a bottle against the wall and cut his wrist with the glass, severing the veins and tendons. He held up the wrist for her to see. 'Look,' he said, 'I am a man. I can stand pain.' Then he walked all the way to the hospital which was about half a mile away.

Several witnesses said that Muldoon was scared of Hawley. Others mentioned that Hawley was dissatisfied with his £10 fee and wanted a share of Muldoon's empire. This, of course, would have been a very possible motive for murder.

I had circulated the registration numbers of the cars driven by Michael Muldoon, his wife Sandra and Kenneth Eighteen to all police forces. But Muldoon saved us the trouble of looking for him by returning to his flat. He first approached two police officers in Stockwell Road under the impression that someone had broken into the flat. He was taken to Brixton police station and then to Loughton where I interviewed him.

He was broad-shouldered with long blond hair, of medium height, a powerful man. But as he was brought into my office, the first thing I noticed was that his left hand was bandaged and there other wounds on his right hand. He said nothing about them at this stage and yet they clearly worried him.

I said that I understood he wanted to tell me all about the death of Hawley. And he replied, 'I don't want to tell you. But I am willing to, if my wife and kids are all right. I want to protect them from Tony.'

He then told me a story about having a drink with Hawley – whom he called Gerry – in his flat on the night of the murder. Then round about two o'clock in the morning, a man called Tony arrived with a girl. They had all been on LSD and red wine, and a fight broke out between Gerry and Tony which ranged throughout the flat.

He said, 'Tony had a long knife like a bayonet in his hand. He also had Gerry's knife.'

Now this was interesting, because Dr Ivy Tuck had

already told me that two different knives were used in the attack on Hawley.

According to Muldoon, Hawley rested for a while after the fight, then left, walking, assisted by Tony and the girl. Muldoon lent them the keys to his wife's car, and all three drove off. Next morning, the keys were back through the letter-box. He was quite definite that he hadn't gone near the car, that Hawley was still alive when he left the flat, and that he had never been to Epping Forest in his entire lifetime.

Several things gave the lie to this story.

Firstly, Hawley's wounds were all grouped over vital areas, back and front – the heart and throat. Dr Tuck stated that no man wounded thus could have walked anywhere. He would have been dead.

Secondly, all the wounds had been inflicted at the same time, thus precluding any suggestion of a second attack having taken place elsewhere.

I asked Muldoon to explain the cuts on his hands and he said, 'That was when I tried to get the knives away from them. I thought I'd been stabbed when I went down.'

He then agreed to be examined by a doctor and for a blood sample to be taken. Again, I called in Dr Tuck.

Muldoon had several bruises on his body and there were traces of green paint on his toes. It matched the new paint in his flat and the residue in the tin found in the alley.

His blood sample grouping revealed: that he had been in the death car – that of Sandra Muldoon; that he had been in Epping Forest, just twelve feet from the body.

Yes, we had a link with those two small bloodstained stones. One carried the dead man's blood, the other Muldoon's. So much for his denials! Quite clearly his damaged hands had betrayed him three times, by dripping blood in the car, in the forest and in Hawley's flat. Remember the bloodstain we found upon the towel. That matched too.

Muldoon's hands were in a shocking state. He had

67

tried to treat them himself with ointment, knowing that had he gone to hospital awkward questions might have been asked. In any event, he was terrified of having them stitched. As we talked, a strange thought came to me. He must have realised that his situation was parlous to say the least. He was on the brink of a murder charge with only the flimsiest of defences. And yet I think he was more worried about his hands than the threat of a life sentence. If ever a man worshipped his own body that man was Michael Muldoon. He was totally narcissistic. And the prospect of having his hands scarred for life was clearly a haunting one.

I noticed that when he signed his name, he did so with his left hand even though this was the more seriously injured one. This interested me, because Dr Tuck believed that many of the stab wounds had been inflicted by a left-handed man.

I had my doubts about the mysterious Tony, but I didn't disregard the possibility that he existed. Many of the people who knew Hawley were convinced that he couldn't have been killed in a fight by any single man. He was too strong, too well versed in violence, to die that way. This theory was given credence by two points: firstly, we knew that two knives had been used in the attack on Hawley; secondly, according to Dr Tuck, even the strongest of men would be exhausted by the task of stabbing a fellow human being eighty-nine times.

Moreover in a murder, as of course in any investigation, you must explore every avenue. So we began our hunt for 'Tony'. When I'd asked Muldoon to describe him, he'd said, 'He's six foot tall, big, with a goatee beard. I think he gets in the Venus Rooms, the Log Cabin and the El Morocco.' We eventually interviewed thirteen 'Tonys' and eliminated them all. And at his trial, Muldoon would admit that the story of Tony and the fight had been a lie. But there was one odd twist to this which has always intrigued me. There was a real-life Tony who fitted this description perfectly. He couldn't possibly have been involved in the murder. His alibi was watertight. However Muldoon did have a very strong grievance against this man. So was it pure coincidence that when asked to describe a fantasy figure, he pictured this one so clearly?

Another little mystery about Muldoon was posed by a remark he made to a police officer during the journey from Stratford Court to Brixton Prison. He said, 'No one believes that I did this, you know. Gerry had a lot of enemies. If they thought I done it, then it should be me who would be worried. Imagine coming out of court and bang, bang, the old shotgun. That would be nice, wouldn't it?'

I would have imagined that underworld enemies of Hawley would have wished to pin a medal on his murderer. Why Muldoon should have believed otherwise is something that has always baffled me.

When we had first heard the name of Kenneth Eighteen, we had suspected it to be an alias. It was so unusual. However, it proved to be real enough. He was a slim, dark-haired young man who was very much under the domination of Muldoon. He took the 'still' shots during the filming of the blue movies and acted as a courier. He told substantially the same story as Muldoon. He was attacked, he said, by someone with a sword and suffered cuts to his hands protecting himself. Then he ran into his own flat. He said he saw Hawley walk out into the street and climb into a car which was then driven off. After that, his main task was to wash the blood off the walls and skirting boards.

Meanwhile, Sandra Muldoon had been arrested in Cardiff. When the car she was driving was first examined, a piece of the fatty tissue from the dead man's stomach was found under the rubber sealing of the offside door.

The car was then sent to London for a more detailed examination. Blood traces were found on the rear seat, rear carpet, front seat mounting hinge and a seat belt. The blood was in two groupings: the dead man's; and Muldoon's. A pattern in body fluid on Hawley's back matched the pattern on the seat belt.

Sandra Muldoon had appeared in several of her husband's blue movies, and had also worked as a striptease dancer at Churchill's, a top London night club. She could look after herself rather well in a man's world and was by no means the submissive partner in the Muldoon marriage.

She told me that on the night Hawley died, he had been taking LSD and was influenced to such an extent that he described tomatoes she was cooking as flying saucers. This, incidentally, I do believe. Several witnesses spoke of Hawley's constant use of drugs. And it would also help to explain how such a strong man had been overcome. The combination of drugs and wine might well have made him sleepy and vulnerable.

She said that she went into Eighteen's flat and slept for about an hour. Then a noise awoke her and she went downstairs to her own flat. She told me, 'There was blood everywhere. It was all up the passage and over the walls and floor. I could smell it, it was awful. It must have been eight pints.'

I asked her why she had chosen that particular number and she said, 'When I was in hospital, I had to have a transfusion and a doctor told me that when blood is changed it takes eight pints and there must have been that much in my passage.'

She also spoke of a mysterious stranger, and although she didn't call him 'Tony,' the description matched that given by her husband. But her answers differed significantly from that point onwards. She had seen Hawley stretched out on the sofa. I asked, 'How was he?' With her head in her hands, she answered, 'I knew he was dead, but I didn't want to make myself believe it.'

She said she had seen Hawley thrown head first into the back of her car.

I asked, 'Was Gerry moving himself?'

'No, he was thrown in.'

'You said earlier you knew he was dead. Did he get in that car himself?'

She started to cry and her voice was muffled as she repeated, 'No, he was dead.'

Some time later, I said, 'Mrs Muldoon, let me put it to you that you, Kenny and your husband killed Gerry and that afterwards you drove them and the body to Epping Forest, where you dumped him.'

She replied, 'They told me I mustn't say anything. Ask them, they should tell the truth.' She sobbed. 'Why did they do it?'

Michael Muldoon, Sandra Muldoon and Kenneth Eighteen were jointly charged with the murder and stood trial at the Old Bailey.

Muldoon changed his story and admitted that 'Tony' had been a pure fabrication. He told the court that he had killed Hawley in self-defence and to protect his wife and children.

According to Muldoon, they had both taken LSD and were under the influence. 'Then Gerry bit me on the back. I heard him growling like an animal. I was trying to talk to him. I was very scared.'

He said that Hawley then began to mount the stairs to attack Sandra Muldoon, and he (Muldoon) tried to prevent this. They each had a knife and were fighting on the stairs.

This, however, was nullified by Dr Tuck's evidence. None of the stab wounds were in an upward direction and none below the navel. His story was therefore an impossibility.

Muldoon was eventually sentenced to life imprisonment for the murder.

The case was described by the judge as 'brilliant detection'. I like to think he was right.

The story was to have one final ironic twist. My officers had delved through all the reels of film seized from Climax Films in a bid to find those which featured Hawley. In the only one found, he was running naked in pursuit of a girl who was also naked. The location: Epping Forest.

CHAPTER NINE

RONAN POINT

'I saw a body spreadeagled and falling from the sky' ... statement of a witness.

It had been one of those hot, steamy nights when sleep is hard to find. It was somewhere around a quarter to six that I heard a rumble like thunder, although there was no sign of a storm. This was followed by firebells and police sirens. It still didn't mean too much, for these are, after all, the commonplace sounds of any big city. I had no means of knowing that the rumble I'd heard had been caused by an explosion at a high-rise block of flats known as Ronan Point – and that the outside walls on the south-east corner from the first to the twenty-second floor had collapsed. It was the morning of 16 May 1968, and I was now serving at East Ham as a Detective Chief Inspector. All of which meant that for the first time in my life, I was able to walk from my home to the station, something of a luxury in my line of work. I arrived at the station at eight-thirty and was told about Ronan Point. So I immediately went to the scene to find out whether CID could be of any assistance.

It was like stepping back in time to the days of the Blitz. I had been home on leave when the Germans launched their first major bombing raid on the London docks. Some of those bombs had landed on the original site of Ronan Point, and walking home late at night with the searchlights still criss-crossing the sky, I'd seen the rubble. Now the rubble was back again – and so seemingly was the war-time spirit. The dockers had come running from the nearby docks, bringing their heavy machinery with them. The dockers have had their critics but there were no critics that day. They were magnificent, burrowing into the rubble, doing everything in their power to find the injured. Eventually they had to be pulled back, as the work was considered too dangerous. The vibrations from the cranes and heavy lifting gear could so easily have brought more of the building tumbling down.

For me, this was an entirely new facet of police work. I had started out as an observer, but soon became involved, for during the initial digging, we had been picking up constant rumours that someone had secreted a quantity of explosives in one of the flats. The theory in some quarters was that this had been the cause of the explosion – and the added fear was that there might be further explosives still stored in the building. I might add that there were reasonable grounds for such a belief.

So I went to Chief Superintendent Porter, the officer in charge of the operation, and asked for permission to bring in explosive experts. I explained that with feelings beginning to run high, it seemed important to check out this theory as quickly as possible. He agreed. So John Yallop, a Home Office scientist with twenty-six years of experience of explosives, came with his own team of experts. The Special Patrol Group operated under his instructions, sliding down ropes without any thought of personal safety. It was my first introduction to the SPG and I was very impressed. This was one of the reasons why I was so ready to enlist their aid in later years during my spell with the Serious Crimes Squad. They never let me down.

One of the conferences I had with John Yallop took place on the twenty-second floor, and provided a very eerie experience. All the power had been switched off, so the lifts weren't operating. We began with quite a climb and then for two hours we talked in a room that was now open to the world. The wind came whistling through and the floor was literally rocking beneath our feet. Heights have never worried me, but you can believe me, I was glad enough to come down. John Yallop was finally able to assure us that the explosion hadn't been caused by an explosive device. He thought that town gas was the much more likely culprit.

The police took eighty-seven statements from witnesses – and thirty-two of the people concerned said that they had been awake at the time. They may have been, like me, finding it hard to sleep in the steamy heat. Or they may have been awoken by what several referred to as a 'drilling' noise and this would seem to have preceded the explosion. Ten of the witnesses mentioned two separate explosions. But according to John Yallop, this is often an illusion. When an explosion vents into the air, the echo is liable to bounce off other buildings and sometimes off low-lying clouds.

A witness from across the road was looking out of her bedroom window at the time of the explosion and stated, 'I saw a body spreadeagled and falling from the sky.' In fact, only four people died at Ronan Point and this was something of a miracle. The block of flats had only recently been completed, and although they had all been allocated, some of the tenants on the very top floors hadn't yet moved in. These included the flats on the 19th, 20th and 21st floors at the damaged corner of the building. If the explosion had taken place a week later, the results could have been horrendous.

It had all been a complete departure from my normal line of work, namely, catching villains. But it had helped to restore my faith in human nature – and I was sure that the experience would stand me in good stead in the years ahead.

CHAPTER TEN

BIRTH OF THE FUNNY FIRM

'I am not determining a point of law – I am restoring tranquillity.' Edmund Burke.

The Krays and the Richardsons had fallen. But now new criminal tsars were rising, anxious to take over their empires of extortion and torture. As the newly-appointed chief superintendent of Scotland Yard's Serious Crime Squad, my brief from the top was 'to combat organised crime carried out by known professional criminals'. Quite an assignment. Especially when I began Day One in command of nothing: no office; no staff; not even a phone to call my own.

True, I could simply have inherited the existing squad. They were obviously fine officers. They had to be. But no, they were too obviously busy on their previous work and wouldn't relish taking on new commitments with someone they didn't know and hadn't worked with before.

However, there were two members of that existing squad whom I was prepared to consider. The wives and girl friends of gangsters tend to get involved in their activities. So therefore a top-class policewoman was high on my priorities.

Sergeant Joyce Cashmore had worked with the previous team. I didn't know anything about her, but I made it my business to find out. Everything I discovered, I liked. She had won an award as the best policewoman of the year. She was described as very dedicated, intelligent, alert and cool in a crisis. I'm glad to say that she hadn't been over-praised. She duly became a very valuable member of my new squad. Good officer, good detective, good friend and well liked by the rest of the team.

The other officer I chose from the previous squad was Sergeant Bill Waite, whose knowledge of the London Underworld was unrivalled. The Records Office at Scotland Yard is famous the world over. But with Bill in my squad, I barely needed to consult it. You only had to mention a name and it was like pressing a computer button. The information just came pouring out. He was my 'Memory Man'. He was subsequently awarded the B.E.M. and I know of no one more deserving.

I spent a lot of time with Bill in those first few days, running through the lists of gangs and gangsters, looking for our first target. However, I think I'd known from the beginning which one it would be. From underworld informants I had learnt of a gang who were openly boasting to their victims that they were taking the place of the Krays, and that they wouldn't make the mistakes the Krays had. This faction became known as the Dixon Gang. Their leader was Phillip Jacobs, a five foot two inch licensee of three East End public houses. He was popularly known as 'Little Caesar'.

He had gone to school with the Krays, but that boyhood link hadn't prevented the twins from approaching Jacobs in 1965 with a demand for protection money. He decided to make a stand. He approached the Dixon brothers, George and Alan, and formed them into a rival unit. Before the inevitable gang warfare broke out, the Krays were arrested and incarcerated. This, of course, left the field clear for the Dixons to build their own empire. And they had been steadily increasing their influence in the East End ever since. They specialised in long firm frauds and protection rackets. George and Alan Dixon, together with their henchmen, had all been connected in some way with the Krays. They were not at this stage as powerful. But I was convinced that if their arrest was delayed for, say, another twelve months, they would pose an equally serious threat to law and order.

So I went to the deputy assistant commissioner, Mr Harold Hudson, and asked for some men. I was told that under the establishment rules, I would have to wait until the existing Serious Crime Squad had been disbanded. Scarcely the best news I'd heard that day.

'In that case,' I said, 'can I borrow some?'

Mr Hudson nodded slowly. 'All right,' he said, 'You can have two from the Flying Squad.'

Again, these weren't the words I'd been hoping to hear. However, there were two Flying Squad officers whom I'd worked with during my Stoke Newington-Caledonian Road days. Two fearless crime fighters, Sergeant John 'Geordie' Corner and Sergeant Tony Stevens. So I borrowed them.

Like most of the men I 'borrowed', they came initially for three months and stayed for three years. It seemed to be the only way in which I'd be allowed to build the kind of squad I needed. Then a few days later, I borrowed two more. Sergeant Colin Ashdown and Sergeant Brendan Byrne. I had worked with them both on the Synagogue Burnings, and knew them to be fearless and scrupulously fair. With these four men, plus Joyce Cashmore and Bill 'Memory Man' Waite, I set out to check the Dixons and their dreams of annexing the Krays' empire. As I was saying – quite an assignment.

From the very beginnning I knew precisely the qualities I needed in my squad.

I wanted *able* men. In other words, good detectives. Because we would need to ferret out the truth in a deceitful world.

I wanted *fearless* men. Because we were bound to encounter threats and pressure along the way. And in this game, you must never be seen to back down. The slightest sign of weakness or indecision will be spotted by professionals for whom such spotting is a stock in trade.

I wanted *honest* men. Because if we were hoping to get the help we needed from both sides of the fence, we needed to instil trust – and to be worthy of that trust. This meant that we had to be above suspicion, with all promises honoured regardless of the cost.

And I wanted *loyal* men. Because we would only achieve our aims by working as a team. Very much a case of united we stand, divided we fall. Loyalty in every walk of life has always been a quality dear to my heart.

I suppose you could sum up by saying simply that I was looking for *men* in the very best sense of that word – not forgetting 'woman' in the person of Joyce Cashmore.

It was also important to me that they shared my own ideals. I once read a quotation by an eighteenth-century statesman and philosopher named Edmund Burke. He had stated, 'I am not determining a point of law – I am restoring tranquillity.'

That reflects my own thoughts upon law and order. I have always believed that in a civilised society, no man should need to walk the streets in fear. And I have never really understood why we are prepared to countenance organised gangs who thrive on terror. The greater the fear they inspire, the more powerful they become. Some people seem to imagine that the existence of the big gangs is inevitable. But that just isn't true. They can all be broken, provided the public – and that includes the lesser criminals upon whom they prey – and the police work together. The hard reality is that at the end of the day, we get the kind of country, the kind of society, that we deserve. I add that we countenanced the permissive society in 1963/4 and I am convinced, as are thousands of my colleagues, that this was the start of the erosion of law and order that used to be so paramount in this country. I will be big-headed and say, 'I know – I was there – I watched it.'

I was determined that my own hand-picked squad would at least pave the way towards that ideal world. In the course of time, they would become famed as 'The Untouchables' and 'The Funny Firm', an underworld tribute to the fact that they were incorruptible.

But for the moment, these were our very early days.

CHAPTER ELEVEN

THE FALL OF LITTLE CAESAR

'Your reign is ending. Wickstead, we will get you.'
Cry from the dock at the Old Bailey.

Michael (Micky) Patrick Flynn was brother-in-law to the Dixons and, by his own admission, the gang's frightener. To say that he was big was a little like saying that Rockefeller was rich or that Capone was bad. He was huge, one of the most formidable men I'd ever seen. The voice went with the man, deep and gravelly. He was telling me that he had left his wife Lynne (the Dixons' sister) and consequently fallen out with the brothers. They had retaliated with a bit of nastiness directed at his sisters. According to Flynn, they had broken the arm of one and threatened the other. Now he wanted to put the matter on a legal footing and he was offering to help me bring down the Dixons. I was pleased, naturally, but puzzled. I would have expected him to take the law into his own hands. The Dixons were big, burly fellows, well versed in violence, but physically they weren't in the same league as Micky Flynn.

I put that point to him and he nodded soberly. He said, 'When I was told about the broken arm, I planned to go round there and break each of the brothers' arms in turn.'

He said this quite matter-of-factly, as though there would have been no great effort involved. And with this man, there probably wouldn't have been.

He paused, held up a hamlike hand and considered it carefully. 'But, you see,' he said, 'I didn't know how far I'd go. So I changed my mind. I wasn't going inside for the likes of them.'

It was then that I understood. The Dixon brothers didn't live under the same roof. Therefore he would have had to make separate visits to achieve his retribution. All of which would have made a clear case of intent. If the Dixons had then made a complaint, we would have had no choice in the matter. We would have had to charge him; and with his almost inhuman strength, it might not have stopped at grievous bodily harm. It could so easily have been manslaughter or even murder.

He then told me the story of how the Dixons had been called in to put pressure on a man who was hoping to gain some control over the Bee Gees pop group. However, having obtained the name, the Dixons decided to 'go it alone' and thus take control themselves. They went to the man's office and took their frightener Flynn with them. He was dressed in a black suit, black shirt, white silk tie and snap-brimmed hat. At pre-arranged times in the conversation, he would join in with little snippets, such as, 'You want an arm broken?' 'A leg off?' 'Or do you want him murdered?'

The man, understandably terrified, lost interest in the group rather quickly. We put all this down in the form of a statement which Flynn signed readily enough. Asked whether he would be prepared to repeat this in the witness box, he shrugged those big shoulders. 'Of course,' he said.

I pointed out to him that somewhere along the line the Dixons were bound to hear about his involvement. 'Now,' I said, 'do you want protection?'

The question seemed to astonish him. 'Me?' he said. 'Need protection? No, I have now put it on a legal footing. You are my instruments. If they come to me, it doesn't become a matter of me attacking them, surely. It becomes one of self-defence. And you have it on record that I am a witness against them – and therefore I'm entitled to defend myself.' Meaning, of course, that (if pushed) he was now in a position to give them a damn-good hiding – legally.

Flynn had provided us with the breakthrough we'd been seeking. We would have got there in the end, but his intervention may well have saved us six months' hard work – and time was important. The Dixons needed to be stopped, and quickly.

Some idea of their arrogance was shown by an incident in the Greyhound public house in Bethnal Green. Two gang members, Michael Young and Michael Bailey, had staged a fight in the bar designed to frighten customers away. This is an age-old story in the East End of London – the first stage in a demand for protection money.

Two off-duty police sergeants happened to be in the pub at the time. They attempted to intervene and were told by Bailey, in no uncertain terms, to get out. He said it was no concern of theirs and he would see that the detective inspector at their station had words with them. Bailey and his mate were 'doing the business', and the officers were not to interfere. Now the two sergeants were young and in any event there were four or five hostiles in the bar. Discretion being the better part of valour, they backed off and left. To their credit, they made notes as soon as they left the pub and then came direct to me. This incident would form the basis for one of the charges against the Dixons. When I eventually questioned Young about these two officers who had tried to stop the fight, he remarked, 'They should have known better, anyway.' The arrogant statement about having words with their detective inspector subsequently turned out to be just that, arrogant words with no basis in fact.

The Dixons made great play of their alleged connections within the police force. And no one was fonder of doing this than Leon Carleton, a club owner and a very oily gentleman. I first met him at his club, The Rebellion, in Ilford. We'd received information that one of our witnesses, a long-time criminal named Bernard Stringer, was going to be seriously harmed that night in the club. Stringer was employed as manager at The Rebellion. We went there in force and stayed until closing time, being very careful to pay for our own drinks. I didn't want Carleton or anybody else to get any ideas about my squad. The Dixon heavies didn't put in an appearance that night, although I learnt that they were in the area.

The following day, two of my sergeants, John Corner and Brendan Byrne, returned to the club. During the course of conversation, Carleton asked them whether I could be 'bought off.' He mentioned sums up to £5,000 and added, 'I've squared up bigger fish than Wickstead. I've got to get him somehow.' He tried to give them presents of whisky and perfume for their wives. But no way. I'd chosen my team too well for this to have any effect at all – beyond it being made the subject of a further charge.

The next time I saw Carleton he was complaining about Bernard Stringer who, he claimed, had made threats against him. This was quite possibly true. There was no love lost between them. But Carleton refused to make any statement concerning these alleged threats. He simply said that he had it all on tape and it would be used for future reference.

He also said that he had taped our own conversations (his and mine) which proved that I had taken bribes. He repeated that allegation later when charged. And at his trial, the judge asked him to produce the tape. He admitted that he hadn't any tapes and that I hadn't taken any bribes. He had just said that in a fit of temper, he told the judge. I wouldn't have described Leon Carleton as one of my favourite men.

In fact, obscure threats were very much his stock in trade. At the club, he had said that he thought I was after him – he wasn't wrong – and then added the customary warning.

I should be very careful, he told me, because a senior officer at Scotland Yard could produce a piece of paper if ever he, Carleton, was arrested. What was supposed to have been on this piece of paper, heaven only knows, because I don't and it was never produced. Again he asked why we couldn't be friends. And after I had made my own position very plain, he finished up by saying that he and I were 'now at war'.

Bernard Stringer told me that, during an argument, Carleton had warned him, 'If you ever laid a finger on me, you would be nicked. Don't you understand? I *am* Scotland Yard.'

Another witness remembered Carleton saying, 'I can take care of the Old Bill (police) in London, but not outside.'

He used these supposed police connections to intimidate people whom he knew had criminal convictions. He threatened to have them arrested by police friends of his, if they didn't do what they were told. Unfortunately there was a suspicion of truth in all this. Two junior officers had been foolish enough to get themselves entangled in Carleton's web. They were investigated and subsequently left the force.

Meanwhile Stringer had become the Dixons' prime

target. On one occasion, sixteen members of the gang armed with various weapons searched the area for him in a cavalcade of cars. They failed to find him on that occasion but then located him a few days later at The Rebellion. Fortunately for Stringer, his eight year-old daughter was by his side. And although he was punched quite severely and told that he was going to 'get done bad', the maiming or killing was not carried out because of the presence of the child.

Stringer was a small man, but he had a very hard way of talking. Mentally, he was tough. Not a man to be easily frightened. Following the threats, it was thought that he got himself a gun; and if the necessity had arisen, I've no doubt he would have used it. He had once been a friend of Phillip Jacobs, but friendships in the underworld can be fragile. When we questioned Jacobs, he shrugged casually as though it was a matter of no real importance. He said, 'Stringer was taking a liberty and had to be seen to.'

Jacobs liked to give the impression that he exerted no control over the Dixon brothers. And there was a temptation to believe that when you saw them together. The Dixons dwarfed Jacobs. But there can be no doubt that he was the dominant force. In this case, money represented power – especially when allied with an agile mind and a ruthless personality. He had left school at the age of fourteen and worked as a waiter in various London restaurants. He had done his National Service in the Royal Air Force and attained the rank of L.A.C. In November 1965, he was married, with, it was said, only ten shillings to his name. And that was the day when his luck changed. His wife's parents gave them the Ship public house in Aylward Street as a wedding present. He prospered rapidly and soon built up a publican's empire by owning the Plough and Harrow, the Bridge and the Royal Oak as well. All of these public houses had one thing in common. They became the meeting places for the 'firm', where various conspiracies were contrived.

Jacobs was frequently to be seen driving through the

East End in a Rolls Royce with the personalised number plates 'PJ' and his current paramour, a Bunny Girl, beside him.

One of the eventual charges against Jacobs was that he had stolen diamonds valued at £14,280. When I first questioned him about this, he asked what were his chances if he told me where they were. When told that I didn't make bargains, he wouldn't tell me. When asked whether he wanted to make a written statement, he replied, 'No, that would bury me, wouldn't it?'

We searched Jacobs' house. We didn't find any diamonds. We hadn't really expected to do so. But we did find something almost equally interesting: a series of tape recordings which he made secretly when talking to members of the gang. Very revealing they were, too. No honour among thieves.

The Dixon brothers, George and Alan, were violent men who had learnt their trade under the Kray regime. However, as personalities they were poles apart. George was taciturn, a scowling, menacing man – the typical East End heavy. Alan, although probably just as dangerous, had an outrageous sense of humour. He seemed incapable of taking anything in the whole wide world seriously. When I asked him about the gang's boast that they were taking over from the Krays, he spread his hands wide. 'All right, Guv'ner,' he said, 'I'll admit it. We've been silly boys. But surely you don't have to grind us down just because we knew the twins.' And when eventually put on trial with the rest of the gang, he cheerfully and ironically applauded my officers when they gave their evidence. In my case, he was even more flattering. He said I deserved an Oscar!

One of our would-be witnesses was doing time in Wandsworth. Obviously, for his sake, I didn't wish to be recognised entering the prison. So I decided to take a leaf out of Chief Superintendent 'Nipper' Read's book. In a similar situation during the Kray inquiries, he had gone through the jail gates disguised as a clergyman. I didn't wish to go quite to those lengths, so I did the next best thing. I went in disguised as a probation officer. I wore glasses and a false beard and did my best to look trendy. I talked to my man in the boiler-room.

I was ready for my first raid. But having only four officers, I asked for help and was given twenty-nine Flying Squad men and sixty others from the Fraud Squad, Criminal intelligence, Divisional CID and uniform branch. The mop-up operation was timed to start at 5.30 a.m., and my team was briefed at 4 a.m. Later, I learned that long before my officers started their job, the *Evening Standard* had the headline prepared, 'Yard swoops on London gangsters.' Somebody had told the newspapers. Even worse, somebody had warned the gangsters that we were coming. There were sarcastic comments from some of them about how late we were in arriving. We were fortunate on this occasion, inasmuch as we arrested most of the principal characters. Only Phillip Jacobs was missing. He was in Spain. We picked him up later when he crept back into the country. But the fact remains that, due to that advance tip-off, things could have gone very wrong. It wasn't a chance I was prepared to take again. That was why on all future raids I used my own squad and the Special Patrol Group exclusively.

Our interviewing techniques with the villains never varied. We played it entirely by the book. We were firm, formal and polite. They were addressed as 'Mister'. We never used Christian names or allowed any familiarity to creep into the conversation. If they became abusive, we reminded them that everything they said was being written down and could later be read out in court. If they refused to answer any questions, I still made a point of asking those questions, my reason being that a jury can always draw its own conclusions, when a defendant declines to answer a perfectly straightforward question. When the interviews were finished, they were allowed to see their wives and families, but never as an inducement, merely the official courtesies. They always had their meals on time. They were never subjected to any violence or overbearing attitudes. In other words, they were treated precisely in the same way that we would have treated any other member of the public who had been brought in for questioning. Their underworld reputations were totally disregarded. I can tell you it dented their ego more than somewhat.

The trial started on 12 April 1972, and went on until 4 July. Each of the accused vigorously defended his case, and by vigorously I mean in every possible way, including, of course, the time-honoured business of attacking the police. No real defence. Just slurs on the police; call them liars and generally do everything to try to blacken them in the hope that some of the jury would believe it.

But the jury convicted all the leading characters. And they received pretty substantial sentences. Phillip Jacobs, Leon Carleton and George Dixon got twelve years each. Alan Dixon got nine years. Michael Young and Michael Bailey, the duo involved in the public house incident, were both jailed for five years.

The judge, Mr Justice O'Connor, told the defendants: 'You have mounted a campaign of vilification during the trial against police officers in the hope of saving your skins. Such activity on your part cannot operate on my mind to increase the sentences I have to pass on you. On the other hand, it does show the nature of your guilt. And it removes entirely such compassion as I would have been willing to show.'

The defendants reacted according to their natures. Jacobs contrived to look astonished. George Dixon scowled. Alan Dixon half-smiled and bowed to the judge. Bailey and Young lowered their heads. And Carleton's mother cried out, 'My son is as innocent as a new-born babe.'

The judge then called me forward and said, 'You and your men deserve the full commendation of the public for bringing this gang to justice. It was a difficult task, thoroughly, honestly, efficiently and fairly discharged.'

At this point, there was an outburst from the dock and

someone shouted, 'The end of your reign in the East End is just beginning. We will get you, Wickstead. We will get you.'

That shout has been variously attributed to Jacobs, Carleton and Alan Dixon. I was looking at the judge, so I don't know – and to tell you the truth, I don't greatly care. Considering the circumstances, it was a foolish remark. Our reign in the East End wasn't about to come to an end. Clearly it was just beginning. The rest of the criminal fraternity realised we were a force to be reckoned with. We couldn't be persuaded to give villains bail when the seriousness of the offence didn't merit it. We couldn't be persuaded to alter our evidence. And we most certainly couldn't be swayed either by threats or bribery.

In the underworld of the East End, we had been given our new name. They were calling us The Untouchables. It pleased me mightily.

CHAPTER TWELVE

GODFATHER OF THE EAST END

'The Tibbs are pure diamonds.' Words of a witness.

James Tibbs was standing outside his greengrocer's shop, and as I walked past, he gave me the sunny smile that was his trademark in the neighbourhood. I wondered whether the smile would have been quite so broad if he'd known that he and his gang were to be the next target for my squad. By an odd twist of fate, my own home in East Ham lay just one hundred and fifty yards from that of the man I intended to bring down. And his brother, George 'Bogey' Tibbs, was a regular at the pub I often used. So I knew the two senior members of the family both by sight and reputation. Many of the people in the area looked upon 'Big Jim' as a modern-day

Robin Hood, a man who robbed the rich to pay the poor. If you're ever in trouble, it was said, go to Jim Tibbs. He'll see you right. But in reality the mantle of Sherwood Forest's bandit hero didn't fit too well upon the broad shoulders of Mr Tibbs. Behind that smiling front, there was a very hard man indeed. The gang he commanded used the boot, knife, hatchet, revolver and shotgun to enforce their will ruthlessly on an area from Romford to Canning Town. His reputation for savagery was so extreme that it put terror into the hearts of rival gangsters. The Richardsons had stayed well clear of Tibbs territory and even the Krays would never cross the iron bridge from Canning Town into the domain of the Tibbs.

Big Jim's sons, John, Robert and Jimmy, formed the hub of the gang. I've heard it said many times that if the father hadn't been such a dominant man, they might well have chosen a different way of life. Jimmy Tibbs, for instance, was a contender for the British middleweight title, a fighter with a big following in the East End. If he had stayed away from this sort of nonsense, he would probably have had both fame and fortune. Still, be that as it may, once committed the sons became very willing practitioners in the art of violence. Other prominent gang members included Michael Machin and Stanley Naylor, both very dangerous men.

The Tibbs were engaged in a long-running feud with the Nicholls brothers, Albert and Terence, and also with Michael Fawcett, a one-time associate of the Krays. The feud had begun on 7 December, 1968, when Albert Nicholls assaulted George 'Bogie' Tibbs in the Steamship public house which was managed by Michael Fawcett's brother, Frederick. The elder Tibbs was punched about the head. His eye was blacked and he lost two teeth.

Three days later, the Tibbs family took their revenge. Ibert Nicholls was attacked outside his mini-cab business late at night. A shotgun blast inflicted terrible injuries to his legs and to the lower part of his abdomen. There were three large jagged lacerations in the scalp and cuts to the face. The tip of his nose was partially severed and he lost the tip of a finger.

Local police officers, who by chance were in the vicinity, arrested the men responsible and several firearms were found in their possession. They were the two brothers, John and Jimmy Tibbs, and another relative. At the Old Bailey, they were acquitted of attempted murder, but sentenced to two years' imprisonment, suspended for three years (would you believe?) and fined £100 each for unlawful wounding and firearm offences. When cases such as this end with this kind of sentence, is it any wonder that gangsters begin to lose respect and fear of the law?

For almost two years, there was an uneasy form of peace. And then on a night in November 1970, Robert Tibbs had his throat cut outside the Rose of Denmark public house. The cut wasn't deep enough to kill, but this was clearly a serious incident. The Tibbs were seemingly sure that Michael Fawcett had been the attacker and there is no doubt that he was involved. The story was confused, with no one (including the Tibbs) wishing to talk to the police. As far as we could gather, Fawcett had intervened when Robert Tibbs threatened one of his friends. Words were exchanged. The men left the pub in a group and during the ensuing fracas, Tibbs was cut. We had no means of knowing whose hand held the knife. When the police approached James Tibbs, the reaction was typical of the man. 'We don't want the police involved,' he said. 'We will deal with this matter in our own way.'

As a matter of record an official complaint alleging that Micky Fawcett had cut Tibbs' throat was made *after* their arrest some two years later. It was fully investigated and submitted to the DPP, but he declined to take any action.

The all too familiar pattern of gang warfare followed. On Christmas Day, John Davies, an associate of Michael Fawcett, was set upon by members of the Tibbs faction while walking alone in a street near his home. He was severely beaten and cut with a knife.

Michael Machin walked into the Steamship public house with a shotgun and fired into the ceiling. Fawcett's brother, the licensee, made no complaint to police.

Edward Machin, the brother of Michael, was in bed on the ground floor of his home when a car pulled up outside. Two shotgun blasts blew out the window and injured him. The car was immediately driven away.

Just over two weeks later, Michael Machin was fired upon by two men armed with shotguns.

The Tibbs kidnapped Ronald Patrick Curtis, a friend of Fawcett, and beat him brutally. Their motive had been to force Curtis to reveal the whereabouts of Fawcett. They learnt nothing.

Then perhaps the most horrifying attack of all took place on Lenny Kersey, another friend of Fawcett. He had referred to the Tibbs as 'dirty pikey bastards'. Pikey is a slang term for gipsy. Stanley Naylor, Michael Machin, John and Jimmy Tibbs armed themselves with knives and an axe. Then they pounced on Kersey as he left his flat in Mile End, slashing repeatedly at his face and body. Kersey's wife Diane was in the flat with a woman friend who was nursing her baby. Hearing the commotion, they ran out into the street to the victim's aid.

Diane Kersey described the scene afterwards. If anyone believes that there is anything remotely glamorous about gang warfare, I suggest that they read her words with care. She said, 'I saw the men hacking at somebody on the ground and tried to stop the horrible thing. Then I saw it was my husband. His face was falling apart. I screamed the place down. My friend also screamed and dropped her baby.'

A doctor later testified that Kersey had over a yard of wounds on his body. He needed one hundred and eighty stitches and a six-pint blood transfusion. During the attack, according to Kersey, someone was shouting repeatedly, 'Kill him, kill him, kill him.' The miracle is that they failed to do so. Later James Tibbs told Kersey, just prior to his court appearance as a witness, 'Get my boys out of trouble. You were hurt bad last time. If you don't go our way, it will be worse next time.' Lenny and Diane Kersey were both too scared to give evidence or even identify anybody in court.

By now the Tibbs had become convinced that they could literally get away with murder. Attacks on the Nicholls continued and the most serious took place outside the Rose of Denmark. Albert and Terence Nicholls were called out of the bar by Naylor and told to get into their car. As soon as they did, the windscreen was smashed with bricks and seven men joined Naylor in an assault with a collection of weapons. The Nicholls fought back as best they could. Albert was stabbed in the arm and leg. Naylor produced a gun, but it was knocked from his hand and picked up by Jimmy Tibbs. Before anything else could happen, the police arrived and the attackers fled.

Terence, the more seriously injured of the Nicholls brothers, was taken to hospital. But while police were talking to Albert, Jimmy Tibbs returned to the scene and drove his car straight at them, causing them to jump for their lives. The already wounded Albert decided to follow his brother to hospital. However, he was stopped on the way by Jimmy Tibbs and Naylor. They forced their way into his car and tried to hit him with a golf club. He managed to throw Tibbs out of the car and then drove off with Naylor alongside, fighting to take over the controls. As they approached the Blackwall Tunnel, Albert leapt out of the car and escaped.

Another friend of Fawcett, George Brett, was shot in the leg. But in the end it was an attempt on the life of Jimmy Tibbs that convinced me it was high time that I intervened personally. Enough was enough. A bomb had been placed under the engine of Tibbs' car and exploded outside a school. His four-year-old son was with him. They escaped injury only because the bomb had been fixed near the radiator. Another two feet further back and they would almost certainly have been killed.

From my point of view, the timing was unfortunate. We were still engaged on the Dixon enquiry and I would naturally have preferred to complete that before moving on to another. But now that the public were quite clearly being endangered, I had no choice. This nonsense had to be stopped.

I still had only a four-man squad, so I wrote out a report for my senior officers and the Home Office which explained that it was impossible to go ahead without reinforcements. I was told I could borrow some more men. But despite my pressing need, I was determined to continue to choose them with care. As far as I was concerned, only the best would do. And that's precisely what I was getting. The best.

Bernie Tighe joined us from the Fraud Squad and was to prove a tower of strength. The complete police officer.

John Lewis, known as The Beatle, arrived around the same time – and formed a close friendship with both Bernie Tighe and Brendan Byrne. John was a very likeable extrovert who is now expounding his very considerable knowledge to students at the Detective Training School.

John 'Fingers' Farley, also known as The Ferret, could have been born to be a policeman. He loved the work. He operated best when the reins were loose. So I would give him a job and let him do it in his own way – quite aware of the fact that I might not see him again that week. He thought the world of his wife Mavis. And I'd know that when he wasn't living up to his name and ferreting out the villains (which he was most of the time), he'd be at home doing the washing for Mavis.

Dave McEnhill was very much in the Farley mould. Our court jester and a man who never made an enemy. Everyone liked Dave. I always thought it a pity that, like Geordie Corner, he never passed a promotion exam. But in Dave's case, I suspect he may have been happier the way he was.

I had picked two of the squad on the memory of first meetings. A few years earlier, I had been on a Board selecting aides to CID. Douglas Gowar had arrived late, but for one of the best of all reasons. His wife had just given birth to their first child. He had come straight from the hospital and he was over the moon. Such emotions might well have disturbed a lesser man's concentration. But not Douglas's. He came through with flying colours. A unanimous decision.

I was sitting on another kind of enquiry when I first saw Colin Evans. A disciplinary enquiry. He had been accused of assaulting a lorry driver. He was very Welsh and very fiery, but there was a fierce honesty about him. He was a man who spoke with his eyes. And it soon became very apparent that the allegation was false. I was most impressed with Colin Evans that day.

Stanley Clegg was another Geordie, volatile and efficient. Borrowed from the Flying Squad and never returned.

Roger Stoodley was an East End officer who enjoyed life. Very witty, absolutely loyal and a good man to have on your side.

I first met Ken Tolbart at East Ham and he became my second-in-command. A very quiet, determined, nice man who could charm the birds out of the trees – and frequently did. During interviews, we developed a tremendous rapport, a kind of telepathy. Very useful when dealing with big-time villains.

Geoff 'Nobby' Wragg and Bob Hind formed an unholy alliance. Hard working, but quite incorrigible. On one occasion, they engineered themselves a trip to the South of France – just a shade deviously but, as it turned out a most necessary enquiry and series of interviews connected with another most serious case. And then, being wise in the ways of men and commanders, they brought me back a present – a plaque from the Sûreté in Monaco. When there were fears that the wife and children of England's football captain, Bobby Moore, might be kidnapped, I gave Nobby Wragg the job of guarding the family. For a while he became part of the Moore household. It was an assignment clearly to his liking. Shortly afterwards he married Bobby's very attractive au pair.

Derek Robinson, known as Big Robbo, and Gerry Runham had come to us on loan from South London. Derek, as his name suggests, was very big and good company. Gerry was pithy, pungent, a first-class exhibits officer.

Terry Brown, as big as Robbo, was the cartoonist's image of a police officer. Big, broad and blustery; so different from his grand passion – fishing. He was never happier than when sitting on a river bank, all alone and in the pouring rain.

Gerry Wiltshire was one of the most tenacious men I ever knew. He just never gave up on a job. If need be, he would wait forever.

Graham Howard was another quiet man. Astute, able, he was always liable to spot the things other men had missed.

Then last, but by no means least, we had another policewoman on the team, Norma Salisbury. She was very much in the mould of Joyce Cashmore – and so, it goes without saying, first-class.

Even with such a squad as this, you still need one more shot in your armoury before you can hope to bring down the gangs. You must learn to use the law as your instrument of justice. This means doing your homework, learning the Judges' Rules; and it also means that you must have ready access to legal guidance whenever the need arises. This was why I made such a point of building a direct bridge between our squad, the office of the DPP and senior Treasury Counsel. The response was wonderful. Both Doylan Williams at the DPP and officers of the Crown such as Michael Corkery, David 'Dai' Tudor-Price and Michael Hill went out of their way to help us. Their door was ever open.

Michael Corkery was the senior prosecuting counsel when each of the three major gangs we had pursued was put on trial. We worked together for four years and so I came to know him well. He was a dedicated professional who always wished to learn everything possible about the background to a case. He would visit the scenes of crimes and work long days. He was also a kind and decent human being we all came to look upon as a friend. Certainly if I was ever in trouble with the law – something I don't really envisage – Michael Corkery would be the man for me. 'Dai' Tudor Price is now His Honour The Common Sergeant of London and has become one of the best of Her Majesties judges.

With this kind of support, we were confident we could do the job. And that job, as far as I was concerned, was to bring down the Tibbs. I believed that there was only one way in which this could be done. We would have to persuade their enemies, the Nicholls, the Kerseys, Michael Fawcett and others, to witness against them. You can accuse me, if you wish, of taking sides – of using one band of villains to break another band. And I wouldn't deny it for a moment. In the twilight world of the gangster, archbishops are thin on the ground. You have to use what you can find – and inevitably that means fellow criminals. And so I had simply asked myself the key question: namely, which faction posed the greatest threat to law and order. The answer to that had to be the Tibbs. They were a highly organised gang. They were becoming steadily more powerful, more ruthless, more ambitious. They were also more wicked and crueller than their opponents. The Nicholls weren't a gang in the accepted sense of the word – more of a loose collection of criminal friends. The same thing could be said about Michael Fawcett and his associates. My decision, incidentally, was agreed and fully endorsed by the DPP. The Tibbs were very anxious to make it appear as though they were the ones under attack. They made great play over the fact that an explosion had occurred at a cafe owned by James Tibbs. Forensic tests proved that the explosion had been caused by nothing more sinister than a gas leak.

Stanley Naylor complained that six bullets had hit his car. I had a look at the photographs of the incident and read the report and sure enough the six bullet holes were there. But if Naylor had been in his car at the time, as he claimed, he would have been a dead man. So I leave you to draw your own conclusions.

In the meantime, we tried to instil trust in our potential witnesses. They were wary of our approaches, but at least they listened. I later discovered that while we had been enquiring about them, they in turn had been asking questions about us. They wanted to know whether we could be trusted, whether the Tibbs faction would be able to bribe us and whether we were totally determined to end this reign of terror in the East End. I am told that they were happy with the answers.

The man I most wanted to talk to was Michael Fawcett, because I had the hunch he could prove to be the key figure in all this. He was regarded with respect by the Nicholls and Kersey; and I had the feeling that the others would follow his lead. So I put out the word in underworld circles that I wished to see him. And finally there was a voice over the phone saying, 'This is Michael Fawcett. I understand you want to talk to me.'

I asked him whether he'd like to come to my office in Tintagel House.

His voice held the caution of the hunted man that he was. 'No, I would prefer to meet you outside Westminster underground station,' he said. 'Could you wait for me there in a car?'

I said, 'Gladly. When will this be?'

'I will ring you half an hour before the meet,' he said, and immediately replaced the receiver.

Two days later, he rang to say he was on the way. Now you have to understand that I'd never so much as clapped eyes on the man before. Knowing that the Tibbs were hunting high and low for him, he had wisely gone to ground. All I knew was his reputation. The Tibbs had painted the picture of a terrible tearaway, the Krays' hatchet man, a madman who had cut the throat of Robert Tibbs on little more than a whim.

I waited for him in the back of a police car just opposite the Houses of Parliament. He came out of the station, glanced with deceptive casualness both ways and then slid quickly into the seat beside me. My first reaction was one of surprise. He stood no more than five foot six. He was slimly built with a boyish face. The voice was quiet. Not exactly what I'd been expecting. And we later discovered that much of the Fawcett legend was based on a myth – largely built up, I suspect, by the Tibbs. It's true that he had been an associate of the Krays, but mainly as a front man in their long firm frauds, never on the violent side of their organisation. He was capable of violence, certainly, and would defend himself vigorously. However, violence with this man would always come as a last resort, and could never be classified as mindless.

We drove slowly down the Embankment and I was content to let him do most of the talking. He was pleasantly direct. He said he had come as a spokesman for the criminal opponents of the Tibbs. They were agreed that if the troubles weren't stopped, somebody sooner or later would be murdered. In fact, it looked as though it could be more than one person.

He confirmed my hunch. 'Don't worry,' he said. 'Now that I've agreed to help you, the others will too.'

In the days that followed I saw a lot of Michael Fawcett and found him to be a very likeable man. However, it soon became clear that if we were really going to bring down the Tibbs, he would have to change his role from that of informer to that of witness. I put the point to him in my office.

I said, 'The decision has to be yours. I'm not going to pressurise you. But I don't believe we can bring them down any other way.'

I could tell by his face that he was shaken. He let the silence drag out and then he nodded slowly. 'Okay,' he said, sounding far from happy. 'If that's the only way, it's the way it will be.'

He was thinking that his life was in even greater jeopardy than it had been before. He was, of course, quite right. It was. This was why Sergeant John Corner was acting as his bodyguard. A strong rapport had grown up between them and I think this played its part in persuading Fawcett to make this decision.

John Corner was in the office with me that day and he began to kid him along. 'You'll only have one trouble at the Old Bailey,' he told him. 'You won't be able to see over the top of the witness box.'

Fawcett responded instantly to his mood. 'You know,' he said, 'this could be my last appearance, so I'd better do it in style. Maybe I'll wear a cape, one of those Batman and Robin things.'

A tense situation had been defused and for the moment fear went away. Fawcett did subsequently go to Spain where he felt a bit safer. But he returned in time for the trial – in his own words, 'to honour my obligation'. And under the fiercest cross-examination, he never faltered. He stood up to it like a man. In fact, he had grown in stature. He was no longer the informant walking in fear of his life. He had taken on the mantle of a prosecutor, determined to see that justice was done and that these wicked men would be put where they belong. If the term 'wicked' sounds fanciful when used by a known villain such as Fawcett, I should explain that it's all a question of degree. The criminal world has its own code, and in the view of the great majority, the Tibbs had transgressed that code. Michael Fawcett had simply become their spokesman. You can be sure it took considerable courage. I had a lot of respect for him and I showed it later by breaking one of my golden rules. Normally I make it clear to criminals who assist the police that I'm grateful for that help, but just the same it doesn't buy them absolution from any future sins. If they should be foolish enough to get into any future trouble, then they are on their own. They mustn't count upon receiving any help from me.

Well, Michael Fawcett did get into trouble and he did ask me, through his defence counsel, for help. And this time, I did give it. I felt that the little man had earned the right. I went along to court and spoke on his behalf. I told the judge what a tower of strength he'd been, not only to us, but in boosting the morale of the other witnesses such as Kersey. I explained that partly as a result of that case, he'd been prevented from earning an honest living. He still spent much of his time looking back over his shoulder. And I'm glad to say that on this occasion, we were able to do him a favour.

We had intended to arrest the Tibbs and their associates sometime in the middle of May 1972. But we then received information from the underworld which forced our hand. The more prominent members of the Tibbs gang, we were told, intended to disappear – probably abroad. Before doing so, they planned to dispose of their criminal opponents, the Nicholls brothers, Kersey and Fawcett.

So during the early hours of Tuesday, 4 April, we made our move. My squad, assisted by a large contingent of officers from the Special Patrol Group, swooped on the homes of the gang members and detained thirty-six men, some of whom were later charged at City Road.

Robert and John Tibbs escaped the initial round-up. Robert subsequently surrendered in the company of his solicitor, while his brother's capture owed much to the varied talents of Detective Constable John 'The Ferret' Farley. We had a tip off that John Tibbs had been seen visiting a certain house; so John Farley took a job on a building site immediately opposite the house. In addition to everything else, he was a qualified carpenter. And after four days, he was rewarded with a sighting of his quarry. The arrest followed within minutes. I often wonder whether he went back to that site for his wages for those four days. I must say that in spite of all the jokes and chaff about him, John Farley was a good detective and well liked by the squad. I am more than pleased to see he is now a Detective Inspector still working in the East End.

The questioning of the suspects was carried out by myself, Detective Chief Inspector Williams, Detective Inspector Ken Tolbart, Detective Sergeant Colin Evans and John Corner, the junior officers, Colin and John, having the most difficult task of recording every word spoken during these interviews. They took place over two whole days and nights almost without a break. It's vital in such cases to have the questions asked as quickly as possible, before the defendants have a chance to prepare their stories. You must remember that we were dealing with experienced criminals, well versed in the art of blocking interrogative questions.

During the four days that the operation lasted, Detective Sergeants Brendan Byrne, Bernard Tighe, John Farley, Douglas Gowar and Roger Stoodley worked a minimum of eighteen hours a day. They searched other addresses, seized more weapons, talked to other would-be witnesses and dispelled their fear of retribution.

At times like this, a good night's sleep looms up as the most valued gift of all. The combined pressures take their toll. I know. By the time the case had finally ended, I'd lost a full stone in weight.

When James Tibbs was brought into my office, the sunny smile had gone. He sat down, flanked by two officers. Then he looked at me. 'Can I see you alone?' he asked.

I shook my head slowly. 'There are no secrets in this squad,' I told him. 'Anything you wish to say can be said in front of them.'

This was clearly the last thing he wished to hear. His face hardened immediately. The Tibbs, like the Dixons, had been on friendly terms with some police officers, and I think this gave them the feeling of being invulnerable. No matter what happened, they told themselves, a deal could be worked out somehow, somewhere. Well, we weren't in the business of making that kind of deal with anyone. And as the interview moved on, the realisation of this came to James Tibbs. His face became harder moment by moment. A far cry from the ever-smiling greengrocer of East Ham.

The other Tibbs were still apparently quite confident. They boasted openly to police officers that, by the time of the trial, we would have no witnesses left. It is strange how often this boast is made. Meanwhile a lot of people in the immediate neighbourhood insisted upon believing that the Tibbs family had been the victims in this whole affair. A witness at the trial would declare that 'the Tibbs are diamonds'. And that wasn't a lonely opinion.

I have heard it said that he would never let any old-age pensioners go hungry and that he was a good family man. This may well have been true. But the fact remains that he encouraged two of his sons and their associates to inflict the most horrible injuries upon Kersey in full view of his wife. Even the most hardened criminals are normally reluctant to attack a man in front of either his wife or children. And not content with this act of butchery, James Tibbs then tried to obtain the £1,000 which Kersey had received from the courts as compensation for his wounds.

My own situation in the neighbourhood had become impossible. There had been a spate of anonymous phone calls, mostly in the middle of the night, threatening that the house would be bombed and that acid would be thrown in my wife's face. Considering some of the madness that had gone before, these had to be taken seriously. There was of course no evidence to show that these threats emanated directly from any of the prisoners. With my wife as hostage to violence, I couldn't afford to ignore them. So I moved home and found a pleasant house, but one which unfortunately needed to be decorated from top to bottom. I wondered if I'd ever find the time to do so. I was still wondering when Saturday came around and glancing up the driveway I spotted my entire off-duty squad advancing, paintbrushes at the ready. They proceeded to do the job in a time that would have put professional decorators to shame. On such occasions, I am not very good at finding the right words, but I think they knew how I felt about this. They had given me a prize above value. I had forged a team to be proud of. And I was. Very proud. And very touched.

Following their trial at the Old Bailey in October, 1972, seven members of the gang were jailed for a total of fifty-eight years. James Tibbs received a sentence of fifteen years. Stanley Naylor was jailed for twelve years, Michael Machin for eleven, Jimmy Tibbs for ten.

The judge, Mr Justice Lawson, told the court: 'Before we rise tonight, I think it is appropriate if I just say this. I

G.—6

do feel myself that the thanks of the public are due to Mr Wickstead and the members of his squad who quite obviously have been confronted with a very difficult task in the preparation and bringing of this case and whose work has resulted in the bringing to justice of people who, according to your verdict, ought to have been brought to justice, as they have been, and I think we owe a debt and the public owes a debt to Mr Wickstead and those who work with him in the detection and running to earth of what are really very serious crimes and possibly potentially much more serious than the crimes which they have in fact, according to your verdict, committed.'

The Commissioner, Sir Robert Mark, commended us. And the Home Secretary, Robert Carr, sent a letter to him asking him to convey thanks and appreciation to myself and the other officers concerned in 'this difficult investigation which had been carried out with a skill and thoroughness which deserved the highest praise'.

This was all very pleasant and very satisfying. But to me the most important point was that some measure of tranquillity had been restored to the streets of the East End. I intended to do everything in my power to make sure that it stayed that way.

CHAPTER THIRTEEN
THE LAMBTON AFFAIR

'I like to believe there is a little foolishness in every man.' Lord Lambton's words, following his resignation as the Minister in charge of the Royal Air Force.

Lord Lambton was strolling along the fifth floor at Scotland Yard. His clothes were immaculate, pure Savile Row. His overcoat was draped loosely over his shoulders and he wore dark glasses. He was the epitome of the English aristocrat, haughty, austere, reserved and seemingly without a care in the world. But I had good reason to believe that this world of his was about to fall apart. Unbeknown to Lord Lambton, we had a picture of him lying on a bed with two prostitutes and reputedly smoking cannabis. We had a tape recording which appeared to confirm that impression. And we also had a copy of a cheque for £50 made out to high-class call girl Norma Levy and signed by Lord Lambton.

I steered him into the office of Deputy Assistant Commissioner Ernie Bond. The Minister in charge of the Royal Air Force had come to see us at our invitation; and our approach would be formal, correct and very polite. Mr Bond invited him to take a seat. But he said, 'No.' He would rather stand. He began to pace up and down the room, his coat still hanging loosely from his shoulders, his manner still haughty. And yet somehow this attitude didn't really seem to ring true.

Mr Bond asked him whether he knew Mrs Norma Levy who sometimes called herself Miss Norma Russell. He admitted quite casually, 'Yes, I have been to bed with her. She's a kind of prostitute.'

Mr Bond cautioned him and asked whether Norma Levy had ever supplied him with drugs. It was then that a marked change came over the man. The haughty manner went away. He sat down in a chair and we saw for the first time, I think, the real Lord Lambton. A rather confused and a very worried man. He must have been aware of the political repercussions. Ten years earlier, the scandal that blew up over War Minister John Profumo's liaison with call-girl Christine Keeler had come close to bringing down the Government. Now in so many ways Lord Lambton's situation was an echo of the one that had gone before. Both men were Service Ministers. Both had access to secret documents. And both had laid themselves open to the threat of blackmail. At that moment, he might well have been remembering something he had written in the London *Evening Standard* ten years earlier. The relevant words: 'In many of this morning's papers there appeared to me to be optimistic forecasts that Mr Profumo's resignation

103

would mark the end of this affair. I greatly regret that I do not believe that this will be the case. It is merely the beginning of another unfortunate chapter which may end heaven knows where.' Dramatic irony indeed!

To his credit, he was absolutely frank with us. He admitted freely that he had shared a bed with two women, Norma Levy and a black girl called Kim. And of Levy, he said, 'I liked her, but she played no important part in my life whatsoever.'

But it wasn't the prostitution angle that primarily concerned us. A sexual transaction freely entered into by a client and a prostitute is not in itself a crime. Drugs were something else again, particularly when a Minister of the Crown was involved. On this subject too, he was entirely frank. He said that he had first smoked cannabis twenty years earlier while in China. When shown the picture of himself smoking on the bed with the two women, he admitted that this might well have been cannabis. The tape recordings contained repeated references to drugs. Questioned about this, Lord Lambton replied, 'This all arises out of my fetish to talk about drugs when I go to bed. It was all a game we played.'

However he was anxious to stress that he had never injected drugs. He very readily stripped off, voluntarily I might add, in the office so that we could examine his arms and legs, and thus verify the point. We did so and, just as he had said, there were no needle marks. He was wearing red flannel underwear, a little rare in this day and age. I made no comment, because the point was no longer necessary. But some of the girls from the call-girl ring interviewed earlier had spoken of an aristocratic client (name unknown to them) who'd worn red flannel underwear. If proof had been needed, this would have been one more link in the chain.

Having got over the initial shock, he really was a most pleasant man. At his invitation we went with him to his house in St John's Wood, so that it could be thoroughly searched. Lord Lambton himself took from a concealed cupboard in the skirting board, a plastic box containing some cannabis resin and a small number of amphetamine tablets. He explained that he had hidden them there to avoid any danger of his children finding them. We then entered his wife's bedroom which had an adjoining bathroom. On a shelf in this bathroom, we found a fawn-coloured purse containing a Walther gas pistol and a tin containing three cartridges.

Lord Lambton was present and I said to him, 'This appears to be a prohibited weapon and I must caution you. Whose is it and where did it come from?'

He said, 'This can be a lonely house for a woman and my wife is easily frightened. We have been burgled a large number of times since we've moved in and I bought her something like this, I think in 1958, somewhere on the Continent I think, but I thought it was lost.'

By then, of course, he had no illusions about his fate. 'I can see this is the end of my political career,' he said quietly. 'I shall resign as soon as I return to my office.'

His resignation was made public the following day, 22 May 1973. And my involvement was heralded by a press statement which said: 'The Prime Minister has personally ordered police to probe vice allegations to avoid any Watergate-type suggestions of a cover-up. Scotland Yard has appointed Mr Bond to keep a watching brief. Investigations will be be carried out by the Serious Crime Squad headed by Mr Wickstead. Up-to-the-minute progress reports are being passed to the Home Secretary and the Director of Public Prosecutions.'

Lord Lambton remained very open. It could be suggested that this was simply the tactic of a wise man – that realising we knew most of the facts, there was no point in holding anything back. I prefer to believe otherwise. All my dealings with him suggested that he was an honest man who valued the truth. It was almost as though he'd said to himself, 'Well, now that I've been caught, let's make the best of it. I'm a member of the English aristocracy. So chin up, chest out, and let's show

105

the world I'm a man.' And to his credit, he did! He never showed any sign of self-pity, although the blow must have been bitter. He didn't attempt to make any excuses or to bemoan his ill-luck in getting caught. Perhaps the nearest he ever came to giving an explanation was when he said, 'I think that people sometimes like variety.' Another time, he said, 'I like to believe there is a little foolishness in every man.'

He was, of course, a very wealthy man. The Lambtons have owned most of Durham since the times of the Norman Conquest. A family curse has been passed on over the centuries. It says, 'No Lambton will die in his bed.' And certainly they appear to have been a strangely ill-fated family. Lord Lambton's elder brother, for instance, committed suicide.

The remarkable feature of his London home was that it had been divided precisely into two halves. Lord Lambton's half was almost spartan in appearance, more befitting a batchelor than a married man. Lady Lambton's half, by contrast, was beautifully furnished and full of female fripperies.

I had to interview Lady Lambton about the Walther pistol which we had found in her bathroom, and on this occasion, I was accompanied by Joyce Cashmore who was then a detective-sergeant. Lady Lambton, if my memory serves me, was wearing a negligee and looking very regal. We said our 'Good Mornings' and I explained why we had come. But before I could say anything else, she turned to her solicitor and said in a languid sort of way, 'Do I really have to talk to *these people?*' I have known more tactful opening lines. The solicitor explained that she would be wise to answer our questions. And she did so, albeit in a somewhat distant fashion. Afterwards the solicitor, a most charming man, took us aside and asked us not to pay too much attention to his client's attitude. I assured him that I wouldn't. It had, after all, been little more than a formality. The Director of Public Prosecutions decided, quite rightly in my opinion, not to pursue the inquiries. The gun was confiscated and that was the end of the matter.

A few days after my first visit to Lord Lambton's house, I had to fly north and serve a summons on him for the possession of cannabis and amphetamines. Sergeant Graham Howard came with me. When we arrived at Newcastle airport, Lord Lambton's chauffeur-driven car was waiting to take us to his country seat, Biddick Hall.

It must have been a difficult day for him. Robin Day and a BBC camera crew had already arrived to film a somewhat bruising question-and-answer session. But it didn't show. Lord Lambton met us at the gates and behaved as though he had all the time in the world. He was politeness personified.

Upon our return to the airport, I rang Scotland Yard and was told that Lord Jellicoe had just resigned as Lord Privy Seal and Leader of the House of Lords. All of which seemed a little sad to me. There was not the slightest link between him and the Norma Levy vice ring. Nor was there any question of a security risk. But he was an honourable man and his conscience persuaded him to follow Lord Lambton's lead, and resign.

A Security Commission, under Lord Diplock, had been set up to study the results of our investigation.

Their report stated that although, as things turned out, security hadn't been compromised, this was still no way for a Minister to conduct himself.

The report declared: 'When, however, we turn to what might have happened if he had continued in the same course of conduct, we consider that a potential risk to security would have been involved such as would have compelled us to recommend that Lord Lambton should be denied further access to classified information. He had admittedly on at least one occasion smoked cannabis when in the company of prostitutes at Norma Levy's flat. We are advised that this is a soft drug which produces changes in mood and perception and gives a feeling of irresponsibility. Hallucinations, too, may be caused. Recorded evidence existed of a conversation which suggested, whether correctly or not, his involvement with other drugs as well and there was photographic evidence of sexual practices which deviated from the normal. This evidence was in the hands of criminals and up for sale. Lord Lambton was thus wide open to blackmail. These two factors, involvement in drugs and vulnerability to blackmail, would have inevitably involved him in disqualification for employment on exceptionally secret work if he had been a Civil Servant subject to positive vetting. In Lord Lambton's case, however, it is not the risk of blackmail that is the dominant factor in the risk. We are wholly convinced that he would never have yielded to any pressure to betray his country's secrets. It is as inconceivable as in the case of Lord Jellicoe.

'The real risk lay in his use of drugs, even though this was confined, as we are prepared to assume it was, to cannabis. Under the influence of this drug we consider that there would be a significant danger of his divulging, without any serious intention of doing so, items of classified information which might be of value to a foreign intelligence service in piecing together, from a number of different sources, a complete picture from which conclusions dangerous to national security could be drawn. We do not suggest that Lord Lambton would consciously commit indiscretions when in his normal state of mind. But we think that there would be a real risk that he might do so in a mood of irresponsibility induced by drugs. We might add here that we are aware of suggestions that other Ministers, besides Lord Lambton, may have been associated with the Levys. We have come across no evidence worthy of credence to suggest that any Minister, other than Lord Lambton, was involved.'

The last time I met Lord Lambton was outside the court after he had pleaded guilty to the possession of cannabis and amphetamines. I had arranged for a car to pick him up from the side entrance, so that he wouldn't have to run the gauntlet of the press. Stylish as ever, he made a point of seeking me out to thank me for the consideration I'd shown him during the course of the investigation.

I suppose I felt a bit sorry for him. But I had surprised myself by coming to like the man.

CHAPTER FOURTEEN

CALL ME MADAM

'He'll kill me if he gets the chance.' Norma Levy.

Norma Levy came off the plane and paused at the top of the steps in the manner of a visiting film star. And watching her, I found it easy to understand how she had become the instrument of Lord Lambton's downfall. She was one of the most strikingly beautiful and elegant women I had ever seen. As she slowly descended the steps, she spotted the waiting battery of press cameras and her expression changed. Suddenly she had the look of a little girl lost, the kind of look that can soften the hardest heart. Once she had reached the tarmac, I moved forward with the newly promoted Detective Inspector Joyce Cashmore and told Norma that I had a warrant for her arrest. As I spoke, I glanced into her eyes and realised that the little-girl-lost bit had all been an act. The eyes were cold, calm and calculating – as hard as granite. Joyce and I guided her through the hordes of photographers and pressmen. She shielded her face, but even then I sensed that she was rather enjoying the situation. She had become the Christine Keeler of the Seventies and she was astute enough to realise that her present notoriety could be exploited to her advantage in the years ahead.

We had a customs check in the police office at Heathrow; and we then took her by car to Tintagel House. Joyce sat beside her in the back of the car and I took the front seat alongside the driver, Sergeant Gowar. Some press cars followed us, weaving their way through the evening traffic. She was intrigued and faintly amused by their attentions. Her only real concern appeared to centre around her husband Colin Levy.

'He'll kill me if he gets the chance,' she said. Just the previous day, Colin Levy had reputedly driven a car at his wife in the little Spanish town of Denia and made repeated attempts to run her down. He had been arrested by the Spanish police and she'd taken the opportunity to flee to England. There was a history of discord between the Levys. And indeed it was this which had been indirectly responsible for bringing down Lord Lambton. When Norma Levy first came to Scotland Yard in April, she was in the midst of yet another feud with her husband Colin. She had come to tell us that he intended to bring drugs into Britain. These, she said, he was going to sell on behalf of James Humphreys. Humphreys, who had been dubbed 'The Porn King,' was at that time wanted by my squad in connection with another matter. Her story was very detailed and mentioned amongst other things a high-powered motor-boat which had been built with a false hull. When Colin Levy did arrive, he was thoroughly searched, but no drugs were found. It was true that he knew Humphreys, but he had no intention of selling drugs for him — and, to the best of our knowledge, Humphreys had never been connected with drug deals.

A few days later, Colin Levy made contact with one of my officers. Having discovered that his wife had shopped him, he spoke freely. He told us that Norma was a call girl, that Lord Lambton was one of her clients and quite possibly a drug user. That was how a domestic dispute came to rock a government.

Now that the dust had settled, Norma Levy was home again and saying to me, 'I want to tell the truth about everything.' She was interviewed at length and a statement, twenty pages long, was taken. She took us step by step along the road that led from Churchill's night club to the position of being the most celebrated call girl in the land. By an odd coincidence, she had been a hostess at the club round about the time when Sandra

Muldoon had been performing her striptease act there. Next she became an escort agency girl, working for the sort of agencies which encouraged their girls to sleep with the clients. And then seeking to get out of the rat race of prostitution, she worked her way into the First Division of the game. She met one madam who blithely informed Norma that she only dealt with Arabs – and that she wasn't fat enough for that side of the trade. She then met a madam who catered for a de luxe call-girl ring which catered for all tastes. It was exclusive – clients by recommendation and personal introduction only. And it was expensive – at least fifty pounds a time. Norma, with her unusual beauty and elegant ways, was clearly ideal for such an elite trade. She went on to the books on a strict business basis. If a fifty-pound fee was involved, ten pounds went to Madam for providing the introduction.

The first two years were spent going to exclusive hotels or luxury apartments to meet the clients. Normally about five a week. Then eventually the clients were sent directly to her own apartment. When Madam introduced Lord Lambton, she called him 'Mr Lucas' and told Norma privately, 'Don't worry about him. His bark is worse than his bite.' After only a few visits, he revealed his true identity freely – seemingly quite oblivious to the risk he was running. But, of course, once you become involved with prostitutes – high class or otherwise – you are always taking a risk. Such girls will have men in their lives – ponces or boy friends or husbands – who, by the very nature of their relationship, will always be tempted to prey upon the clients. Colin Levy was just such a man. He had a prison record. He was unemployed. He was short of funds. And he was drinking heavily. On one occasion when Norma was waiting for Lord Lambton, Colin became so drunk that she locked him in the adjoining bedroom. Lord Lambton arrived a few minutes later and was duly entertained, blissfully unaware of the fact that the husband was literally only yards away from him. So when Levy found a cheque signed by Lord

Lambton (and realised for the first time the identity of the man), the temptation was too strong. He and an associate (who also had a criminal record) decided to sell the story to the press. They set up the most elaborate camera trap with the aid of a wardrobe, smuggled a photographer into the apartment and secretly took a series of pictures – including that very compromising one of Lord Lambton in bed with the two girls and supposedly smoking cannabis.

Norma told me that she hadn't known the pictures were being taken, and this may well have been true. The trap could have been set up very simply while she was out of the flat. Armed with the pictures and tape recordings, Colin Levy and his associate then visited Fleet Street and asked for a fee of thirty thousand pounds. They didn't get it. Instead their evidence ended up in the hands of the police.

The presiding genius behind the call-girl ring was a very rich woman with several properties in London – all, as she said, given to her by 'a rich friend'. She had displayed a certain talent in building up this little empire. The girls, for instance, were a very different type to the average prostitute. They were often models, wives, secretaries, students and teachers – with one thing in common. They were in debt. Through her remarkable social contacts, she would ascertain the client's likes, dislikes and other needs, then introduce him to the girl she considered most suitable. Their addresses and phone numbers were shown, with their nationality, and their colouring – blonde, dark, fair, red. New customers would be given an idea of what they were getting for their money. Old customers could ring the changes. When Madam was on holiday – or, in one case, in hospital – the ring would be run by either Norma Levy or Rocha, a six-foot German Amazon who was a favourite of 'specialist clients'.

I found Madam co-operative, but very antagonistic. She contended that she was simply supplying a service – and that the police had no right to interfere.

Unfortunately for her, the law thought otherwise. Once you exercise influence for gain over prostitutes, you are committing an offence. She was subsequently found guilty and fined two hundred pounds. Rocha was fined one hundred pounds for a similar offence. And Norma Levy, who had been charged 'for attempting to procure a woman to become a common prostitute', was fined £225. This was the sort of sum that Norma, while engaged in her chosen trade, could have expected to earn in a couple of days. But to us, this was really incidental. The Serious Crime Squad had no intention of getting into the business of arresting prostitutes. Our only interest in this elite call-girl ring centered around the question of national security. Ever since the Lambton Affair surfaced, there had been a series of rumours about other Cabinet ministers being involved. And this was something that needed to be checked out very carefully before the investigation could finally be closed. We did find lists of the clients who had used the ring – and many of them were household names. However none of them posed the slightest threat to security and so were no concern of ours. Still, as you can imagine, our enquiries had created some alarm in certain quarters. I still to this day have a quiet chuckle to myself when I see certain familiar faces and think of the very special 'services' rendered to them.

I remember a particularly anxious phone call from a prominent member of the aristocracy who had been a customer of the ring.

He said that he understood Mr Bond and I wanted to see him.

I replied very politely indeed, 'No, sir, we do not want to see you.'

Back came the reply. 'Well, I certainly don't bloody well want to see you' – and crash went the phone.

The Lambton Affair left a trail of wreckage in its wake. Two basically good men, Lord Lambton and Lord Jellicoe, had their political careers ended. Colin Levy spent time in a Spanish jail. Madam had her vice ring broken. And I've no doubt that some of the clients suffered domestic disasters.

There were a lot of losers and only one winner. Norma Levy. She alone gained some measure of profit from all these happenings. She divorced Colin Levy, remarried an American and set up home in Fort Lauderdale, Florida. Then with her new-found fame, she made constant headlines.

The widow of Indonesia's President Sukarno started a libel action over her book *I, Norma Levy*.

A friend jumped to her death from an eighth-floor window while writing another Norma Levy book.

She was alleged to have masterminded group sex orgies in a private Boeing 707 as it flew high over the Atlantic.

And, shades of the London vice ring, she was accused of setting up an elite call-girl ring in that rich man's paradise known as Miami Beach.

Norma Levy may have been many things. But of one thing you can be sure. She was never a Little Girl lost. This was a bright-eyed and bushy-tailed lady who knew precisely where she wanted to go.

CHAPTER FIFTEEN

RAIDING THE SCHEHERAZADE

'You will never get your witnesses.' Bernard Silver's words when charged.

The two men sharing a quiet room with me in the countryside beyond the city were big and burly. They were also scared. Very scared. They had good reason to be. They were giving me the information which would help to bring down The Syndicate, the multi-million pound Mafia-style vice organisation which had ruled Soho for eighteen years. And if their part in this had become known, they would virtually have signed their own death warrants. Even today, if the news leaked, they would be in deadly peril. This is why they must, and shall, remain anonymous.

Having restored a degree of tranquillity to the streets of the East End, we had been widening our sphere. And perhaps inevitably we had been drawn into Soho, London's so-called square mile of sin. In February, 1973, my squad had arrested associates of James Humphreys, labelled the Porn King, for an attack upon his wife's lover. During that investigation, we had learned something about vice in the West End, and of the shadowy figures, almost exclusively Maltese, who controlled it. We were told that they had become so rich and so powerful that they considered themselves beyond the reach of the law.

I am sorry to say that they had been encouraged in that belief by the existence of a few bent coppers. Although the vast majority of West End police officers were good, honest men, they had a scattering of rotten apples within their ranks. Vice pedlars have a peculiar talent for making contact with such officers. Let me make it quite clear that due to enquiries within the force, these were soon identified and rooted out.

Now most professional criminals have a poor opinion of those engaged in vice. When they are seeking for words of abuse, that of 'ponce' comes high on the list. So I have no doubt that, in the normal course of events, the police would have been given enough underworld information to have curbed The Syndicate. But once you have widespread rumours of bribery and corruption, all this changes. The would-be informant no longer knows which officers can be trusted. And with The Syndicate involved, no one could afford to make a mistake such as that. Like the Mafia whom they aped, they had a full quota of hit men and frighteners.

This is why I took it as a compliment when my two informants were prepared to trust me. They had checked the track record of both the Serious Crime Squad and myself – and found it to be straight all the way along the line. The two men were on remand and so cautious that they wouldn't even tell their own legal representatives why they wished to see me. They wouldn't meet me in London, so I suggested a police station outside. To guarantee their safety, I insisted that they should be escorted by officers of my own squad, their legal advisors be told, and that no one else should be involved.

Eventually we had three meetings, each lasting for several hours. I was given the names I needed: Bernard Silver, Frank Mifsud, Emmanuel Bartolo, Emmanuel Coleiro, Joseph Mifsud, Victor Micallef, Frank Melito, and others. Yes, the Board of Directors of The Syndicate. I learned too, the addresses of houses and other properties owned by them. Particularly valuable was a cataloguing of the enemies The Syndicate had made during the years they had been in business, and of their victims. They also gave me background details about the murder – in 1956 – of a gangster, Tommy 'Scarface' Smithson. Briefly, the story I was told was that he was blackmailing certain members of The Syndicate and, as they were about to take over the West End vice empire of the Messina brothers, they couldn't afford to show any sign of weakness. Therefore, Smithson 'had to go'. Two hit men, Philip Ellul, an American citizen and Victor Spampinato, a Maltese, had been hired to do the killing. Ellul had subsequently been found guilty and sentenced to death. On the eve of his execution, his sentence had been commuted to one of imprisonment for life. He had already been freed and returned to the United States. Spampinato had been found not guilty. But when my men caught up with him in Malta, he admitted freely that our informants were right and the jury wrong. He had played his full part in the murder of Smithson. But, for me, the most interesting feature of all this was The Syndicate's involvement. The murder had taken place in a call-girl's flat in Kilburn (some three miles from Soho) and the police at the time had assumed that this was the outcome of a personal feud.

My informants also told me that Ellul and Spampinato were angry and bitter. They hadn't received their blood money. In other words, the contract on Smithson hadn't been honoured. Bitter and angry men are often prepared to talk to the police. And I knew that if they were prepared to talk to me and take a stand, The Syndicate's reign would at long last come to an end.

They had first come to power in the early fifties when they took over the empire of those vice czars, the Messina brothers. The Messinas had variously fled, been jailed or deported, leaving the proverbial pot of gold in their wake. The existing London gangs such as those of Billy Hill, Jack 'Spot' Comer and others, weren't qualified to run that kind of business. Vice is a very specialised form of crime. You need men who can acquire property in the right places and at the right prices. You need men who can recruit and organise the girls. You need rent collectors. And you need a small army of frighteners to make sure that the girls and the collectors stay honest.

The two premier leaders of The Syndicate, Bernie Silvers and Frank Mifsud, had already been operating prostitutes, brothels and gaming clubs in the East End of London – particularly in the Brick Lane area of Stepney. They also had a toe hold in Soho, a strip club in Brewer Street, with four prostitutes operating from above it. With the departure of the Messinas, they immediately started to buy up Soho properties through nominees.

The Syndicate lieutenants at that time included Anthony Mangion, Emmanuel Coleiro, Emmanuel Bartolo and Tony Micallef. But Mifsud and Silver were the two bosses without a doubt, and both millionaires.

Mifsud, a former Maltese traffic policeman, had created a considerable aura of fear throughout Soho. Eighteen stone and known as 'Big Frank,' he was a totally ruthless individual. He had arranged numerous beatings of men in the past. And the simple message 'Big Frank wants to see you' was apt to strike terror into the hearts of even the hardest men. His role in the organisation was to control the activities of the Maltese collectors and strip club managers.

Silver, an East End Jew, was the only member of the hierarchy who wasn't Maltese. He was responsible for the recruiting and placing of prostitutes. He had also gone out of his way to make friends with police officers of varying ranks, so that he could get early warnings of any planned raids. He did have parallels with Phillip Jacobs inasmuch as they were both Jewish gang leaders, both drove a Rolls Royce and both had a Bunny Girl mistress. But that was where the similarity began and ended. Silver was a much more formidable force, every bit as ruthless as Mifsud, a thoroughly evil man.

Soon after taking command of the Serious Crime Squad, I had summoned Silver to Tintagel House for a meeting. I had heard that he was either associating actively with a certain London gang or conversely that he was paying them protection money.

I had been warned that one of his standard ploys when pressed by police officers was to allege subsequently that they had asked him for money. However, as I was seeing him in the nature of an informant, I took my own precautions by having Joyce Cashmore present during the interview which was also secretly taped. He was medium-sized, quite good looking and very, very sure of himself. He clearly regarded me as a country copper who would be no match at all for him in a battle of wits. His police connections were so powerful in those days that I think he really did believe himself to be inviolate, certainly beyond the reach of poor old plodding coppers such as I.

The Syndicate prostitutes were organised on a military basis. One girl would run a flat between 1 p.m. and 7 p.m. That was the early turn. From her The Syndicate would collect over one hundred pounds per week. Another girl, using the same premises, took over for the late turn, ending her shift at two in the morning. From her, The Syndicate would collect on average one hundred and eighty pounds per week. All of which meant an income of near enough three hundred pounds a week from one flat with no overheads and no tax to worry about. The girls would clock on for their shifts dead on time, and leave equally promptly. Their masters liked it that way.

The sleazy strip clubs and the clip joints were doubly important to The Syndicate. They provided a source of high revenue — the strip clubs ran an average of six shows a day with the same girls appearing at maybe half a dozen clubs on the same day — and they also brought in the clients for the prostitutes. It was no coincidence that the flats above the clubs were occupied almost exclusively by Syndicate girls.

As always when attempting to break a gang, our main task lay in persuading witnesses to make statements — and then to stay loyal to the statements they'd made. The second part of that task often proved to be more difficult than the first.

Most of our prospective witnesses were in Malta. So I sent three detective sergeants — Bernard Tighe, Stan Clegg and John Lewis — to the island. Officially they were on holiday, just using up part of their annual leave. I was anxious not to alert The Syndicate until the last possible moment. Amongst others, they spoke to Victor Spampinato who gave us a valuable statement.

But news travels fast in the underworld; and by the time my sergeants returned to London, The Syndicate was already taking steps to silence our witnesses. One man who had spoken to us in Malta was found in the street with a fractured skull, a broken arm and cracked ribs.

George Caruana was another important witness, because it was in his house that Smithson had been murdered. There had been three separate attempts on Caruana's life. On the last occasion, his car had been blown up. He had left the country in a hurry, and was said to be with his wife doing a strip cabaret act in Hamburg. We had a tip-off that two of The Syndicate's hatchet men were already searching for Caruana. So

Bernard Tighe took off again, this time with Sergeant Terry Brown. With the help of the German police, they located Caruana. The club was then ringed by armed German policemen. Good intentions, but somewhat more dramatic than I would have wished.

Still Caruana did agree to help us. He returned to England, made an invaluable statement, and subsequently went to Malta. He then sold his allegiance and went back on his word to us. This was to become a familiar pattern.

Another of our witnesses, Frank Dyer (Maltese despite that English-sounding name), was kidnapped on the streets of London. A band of men seized him and threw him into a van. After a ten-minute journey, he was taken to a basement flat, beaten and tied to a chair. A gun was held to his head and he was ordered to give precise details of everything he'd told the police. Before further harm could befall him, a telephone call was received from one of The Syndicate leaders. As a result of that call, he was released, taken back to Soho and given an apology. It had all been a mistake, he was told.

Still, despite all these bids to stop us, we had gathered enough evidence by October 1973 to swoop on The Syndicate. The fourth was to be the day and half past one in the morning the time. But on the late afternoon of the third, my officers reported, 'The streets are empty. Our birds have flown.' Certainly the top brass had gone. Bernie Silver had set off on a European holiday. Most of his leading henchmen had returned hastily to Malta, their native land.

Our plans for an early-morning swoop were abandoned instantly. It was probably the most disappointing moment of my entire career. Not because we had failed to net The Syndicate. I was already looking ahead, convinced that there would be another day. All I had to do was wait, keep a low profile and they would return. No, I was disappointed because I now knew that I had a traitor in my own camp. As the squad had been founded upon trust, the concept of total loyalty one to another, this came as a terrible blow. The only consolation was that I knew the identity of the traitor beyond all doubt. I couldn't take any disciplinary action against this one rotten apple in the barrel, there was no evidence as such anyway and it would have been a hard thing to prove in black and white. I simply had him transferred. We were once more the Untouchables. We strengthened our security still further by moving our headquarters to Limehouse. This suited my purposes well. I was back in the East End where I had always felt most at home. We had taken over a self-contained block which had just the single entrance. We could thus control movements in and out completely. And next door we had Limehouse police station, very convenient for charging purposes. All in all, an operational officer's paradise.

Meanwhile I had gone to court and been through the motions of having the search warrants withdrawn, in assumed anger. In fact, no warrants were withdrawn, quite the reverse. With the knowledge of the Director of Public Prosecutions, and the co-operation of the Marlborough Street magistrate and his chief clerk, extra ones were obtained – including arrest warrants for incitement to murder Smithson. I then enlisted the aid of the press and persuaded them to print stories with headlines such as 'The Raid That Never Was.' All such stories stressed the point that all the work of the Serious Crime Squad had been wasted – and that the entire operation mounted against The Syndicate was being abandoned. I further underlined that message by mounting a successful operation against a pornographic book empire in the West End.

The Syndicate were now convinced that my true target was porn, not vice. So in December 1973, the Board of Directors started to return to London. On December 30, a most auspicious day, I had been informed that morning that I had been awarded the Queens Police Medal in the New Year Honours List and now Bernie Silver and his girl friend Kathleen Ferguson were spotted entering a London hotel by Bernard Tighe and John Lewis. As they left, both were arrested and taken to Limehouse.

I immediately reorganised the earlier frustrated operation. And in the early hours of that same morning, we raided the Scheherazade Club, the social headquarters of The Syndicate. As we approached, we were spotted by one of Silver's minions. He started to run back towards the club in a bid to warn his friends. But Bernie Tighe downed him with a flying tackle.

As we entered the club, a buxom blonde was singing. Bernie Tighe stepped on to the stage and silenced the band. He also silenced the blonde most politely. Then he announced that a raid was taking place and handed the microphone to me. I explained who I was and asked everyone to kindly remain seated.

A little light relief came when a customer asked his friend how he was enjoying the show so far. 'Rubbish,' was the reply. Even some of the policemen smiled.

It was obvious that we couldn't carry out our identifications and interrogations at the club. So I gave orders that everyone present should be treated as suspects and taken to Limehouse where they could be vetted. Convoys of police vehicles journeyed between Soho and Limehouse. The station had never been so full. We even took the band and they proceded to give an impromptu concert in the charge room while they were waiting.

I am often asked why I didn't take all these people to the nearby police stations in the West End. I suppose my thinking was partly influenced by the fact that I knew The Syndicate had a few police friends in the area. But the main reason was more basic. I had always been at heart an East End copper. This was my home, the part of London that I understood. I had total control over my own manor. At Limehouse, no one would approach the suspects without my knowledge. This I could guarantee.

While we had been raiding the Scheherazade, another one hundred and fifty officers rounded up the rest of the suspects at their homes. Only one big fish escaped our net: Frank Mifsud. He had been living in a terraced house in Dublin, with the local police keeping casual observation on our behalf. When the balloon went up, I asked them to arrest him. But he had gone.

Emmanuel Bartolo was one of the key figures in this vice empire, because he either owned or controlled a vast number of the flats used by the prostitutes. I found him to be a beefy, obsequious man anxious to ingratiate himself. He was known throughout the criminal fraternity of London as 'The Landlord'.

When I asked him how he had been given such a tag, he beamed widely. 'All Maltese have nicknames,' he said.

But wasn't it true that he let flats to girls? He shrugged and gave me the addresses of two houses he owned in North London – clearly the two that were the furthest away from Soho. He seemed shaken when he realised that I had the addresses of his other properties. And although his English was fluent, he became increasingly Maltese in both mannerisms and attitude as the interview progressed.

He shied away from the question, 'Do you pay income tax?' by saying, 'I think I do.' And then no doubt realising how naive this sounded, he added hastily, 'My brother submits the returns for me.'

He did admit that a 'pool' of money had been raised to pay for the kidnapping of Frank Dyer. But when I asked him whether he had contributed to that pool, his smile became positively oily.

'Sir, please,' he protested. 'I'm not a violent man.'

In the meantime, Bernie Silver's solicitor had arrived at Limehouse. He had placed a tape recorder on the front counter and insisted that he be allowed to see his client. I was sent for and told him politely that he couldn't. Quite naturally he became indignant, but I pointed out that my authority for this was covered by the Judges Rules. These rules state that persons in custody should be allowed to see a solicitor 'provided that no unnecessary delay or hinderance is caused to the process of investigation or the administration of justice.' You see, a prisoner may well ask for messages to be given.

And in all innocence, the solicitor may do this. But those messages can result in the arrest of criminal colleagues being impeded, valuable evidence being lost and, in some cases, stolen property being disposed of. I couldn't blame this solicitor for making a firm stand. I expect a solicitor (or for that matter, a barrister) to do his very best for his client. I wouldn't have it otherwise. And I was on good terms with a large number of solicitors, senior QCs and counsel who had frequently given me a hard time in court. We were on good terms, because we both knew that the other man was simply doing his job. There was nothing personal about it.

Bernie Silver's girl-friend, Kathleen Ferguson, didn't play any part in our future enquiries. But at this stage, we had no means of knowing whether she was actively involved in any of his operations. Sergeant Norma Salisbury interviewed her and perhaps the most interesting point to emerge from this was that Silver didn't seem to have a single friend in the whole wide world. Associates, yes. Friends, no. I can only assume that in his line of work, friends were a luxury he just couldn't afford. He had too much to hide.

In those early hours of the morning, I found Silver remarkably calm, cool and collected. I offered him a cup of tea which he accepted. Then, knowing that he had just returned from France, I asked him where his passport might be.

'I'm not sure,' he said. 'It's either in my flat or with my solicitor.'

This, of course, suggested that he must have seen his solicitor since his return. I wanted to know why, and at this, he half-shrugged. 'Well,' he said, 'I knew you were after me.'

I read out the warrant and he looked at me levelly, saying, 'You don't expect me to plead guilty, do you?' And then he added almost conversationally, 'You know, you'll never get your witnesses.'

I let the silence drag out and finally he said, 'You've cautioned me. This is serious. I don't have to answer

124

your questions.'

Well, it was serious. He was quite right about that. I went ahead and asked the questions just the same, as I always do in such circumstances. A jury is entitled to draw its own conclusions as to why a man chooses to reply, 'No comment,' when faced with a perfectly straightforward query.

During the interview, I had been studying him closely. Compared to most gang leaders, he looked reasonably civilised on the surface. But just the same I gained the clear impression that he could be a very dangerous man to cross.

In his eyes, I think, I was still the country copper, still no match for his superior intelligence. He had been carrying everything before him for so long that he just couldn't believe the empire was about to tumble. However, he was a little bit more wary than before, a shade more respectful.

CHAPTER SIXTEEN

WITH THE FBI

'Are you the Grey Fox?' First question from an informer in New York.

Lieutenant Dan Guiney of the New York Police Force drew his revolver, tapped on the door and called out, 'Police.' There was only silence from within. Guiney gestured to me to move back a step out of the possible line of fire, and tapped again. As is common in American cities, the door had a peep hatch. After repeated knockings, it opened and a nose and eye appeared.

Without more ado, Guiney stuck the gun barrel through the hatch and said, 'You open the god-damn door when the Police Department knocks.'

I had come to New York with Sergeant Derek Robinson – 'Big Robbo' to the squad – in a bid to find

Philip Ellul, the convicted murderer of London gangster, Tommy 'Scarface' Smithson. We had been told that a man called Ellul lived at this address and fitted the description. It was a false alarm. Eventually when the door opened, we found a frightened Puerto Rican family who'd had the misfortune to have a Maltese ancestor whose name was Ellul. They had no connection whatsoever with our man.

We had been given three officers to work with – FBI agents Tony Leoni and Bob Quinn, and New York policeman Dan Guiney. We just couldn't have hoped for better men. Leoni and Quinn had met us at the airport and my first impression was that they looked more like business convention types than investigators of serious crime. But I didn't doubt their competence for a moment. As their records showed, they were first-class men in every way – and once the ice had been broken, very friendly ones too. They went out of their way to make us feel at home.

Dan Guiney headed a special branch of criminal intelligence in the city and used a warehouse as a 'front' for his headquarters. He was already a police legend. He had been shot seven times and on each of those seven occasions, he had still carried on and made his arrest. He was, I think, one of the happiest men I've ever met. A man who literally seemed to enjoy every single moment of every single day. I mentioned this to a friend of his who said, 'I guess Dan's been so close to death so many times that life smells extra sweet.' The friend could well be right.

I was anxious that these three Americans should understand why the finding of Ellul was so important to our case. I explained this at some length. I also told them why I believed that for the first time in his life, Ellul might be willing to co-operate with the police. The story, given to us by underworld informers, was that following the shooting of Smithson, Ellul and Spampinato had fled to Manchester and gone into hiding. A few days later, they received a message from The Syndicate, saying:

126

'Surrender yourselves to the police. We have made a deal. The charge will be reduced to manslaughter. After you have completed your sentence, you will be well rewarded. You will never need to work again.' Well, they did surrender to the police; and, of course, there was no deal. Outside of the movies, such deals just don't exist – and both men must have been very naive to believe otherwise. It was a mistake that nearly cost Ellul his life. You can imagine his feelings in the death cell with the days moving by. Betrayed and yet powerless to do anything about it. A late reprieve saved him from the gallows. But that kind of experience is liable to put its mark upon a man. And I'm sure it put its mark on Ellul. He was a lonesome, brooding sort of a man who preferred his own company. Not an easy man to talk to. He eventually served eleven years and then came to London to collect that promised reward. He was received by several of The Syndicate leaders. When he asked for his money, sixpence was thrown upon the floor. He was told to pick it up.

He was escorted to Petty France to pick up his passport, and then to Heathrow. The parting message from The Syndicate was: 'Don't ever come back. If you do, we have a pair of concrete boots waiting for you.' In other words, he would be shot, put in a barrel of cement and dumped into the Thames. It sounds melodramatic. Still, I suspect that the threat was real enough. Ellul had never revealed the name of the man, or men, who had hired him to kill Smithson. He had kept that secret well, but nevertheless it was still a secret, and one that, if told, could destroy The Syndicate. He was a danger they couldn't afford. They wanted him as far away from London as possible.

Now, this was the story we had picked up from underworld sources. A story that I had no means of proving in a court of law. Still, it did match up with several known facts. Ellul had left London in a considerable hurry. He was reputed to be in dire financial straits. And he had shown no desire whatsoever to return to Soho where, due to his line of work, he had enjoyed a comfortable lifestyle.

For both Derek Robinson and myself, New York was a new experience. And being policemen, our chief curiosity centered around the policing methods of the city. We decided to take a look around the police station closest to our hotel. As we walked in, we were confronted by a veritable Amazon of a policewoman. She was six feet tall and three feet wide.

The biggest .45 revolver I've ever seen dangled from her belt. And judging by her expression, it wasn't just there for show. This was one girl who would never need any special protection from male colleagues when the going got rough. We explained that we were London police officers and produced our warrant cards to prove it. She studied them slowly. Warrant cards or not, no one was getting past this guardian of the law in a hurry.

She looked at me. 'Didn't I see you on television the other night?' she asked.

I nodded. She smiled and suddenly she was a different girl entirely, pleasant, friendly and only too anxious to help. The change was remarkable.

We were shown up to the detective section and the whole place smelt of urine and sweat. A grizzled sergeant explained, 'We have just got rid of forty-five prisoners.'

The scene could have come straight out of Kojak. Three sides of the room were a cage with a few prisoners still behind the bars. The detectives were a veritable United Nations, a mix of all the various races who have made America their home. I noticed that all the typewriters were secured to the tables — and that tables and chairs were fitted with castors. When a detective wanted to interview a prisoner, he just needed to push with his feet — and his table, typewriter and chair would be positioned beside the bars. A very commonsense way of doing things.

An Irishman, with a brogue that hadn't been changed one whit by time or distance, explained, 'We haven't got time for the refinements that you may have in London.'

The interest in policing methods was clearly mutual. They were particularly interested in the stop, detain and search powers used in Britain. And they just couldn't understand how policemen could walk unarmed on the streets of London.

I did my best to explain our philosophy on the subject. I said, 'Only a very small minority of British criminals carry guns. But we believe that if the police were armed, that situation would change. Most of the villains would be armed too.'

A big fellow with a streak of grey in his hair, a thoughtful sort of man, put the American point of view. 'Just supposing it was the other way around, as it is here in New York. The criminals are already carrying guns. What would you do then?'

I could only suggest that the basic problem lay with the constitution of their country which made it all too easy for its citizens to own guns.

The following day, I had another instance of the American police officer's reliance upon firearms. I was in a car with Dan Guiney when a call came over the radio. An officer was being attacked and in need of assistance. Guiney immediately switched direction, heading for the trouble spot. And instinctively the guns came out, ready for use.

It proved to be another false alarm, but it nevertheless served to underline a basic truth. Policemen of the Western World come from the same mould, regardless of differing uniforms and regulations. They look after their own. Once the call goes out that a policeman is in trouble, every officer within reach wants to come to his aid – and in a hurry! I was in New York, but I was remembering a night in Hampstead when a young PC had supposedly been in need of assistance. Three thousand miles and almost thirty years separated the two happenings. But the story was the same.

At one time in New York, I did feel as though I'd been caught up in a Hollywood gangster movie. A man phoned and said he wanted to talk to me alone. The local police or the FBI mustn't be involved. So we arranged to meet that same afternoon. I would be waiting for him in a car in a Manhattan Square. Dan Guiney wanted me to carry a gun. 'You could be a sitting duck out there,' he said. But you can't change the habits of a lifetime overnight. So there were no guns for me. However, while I was waiting, I glanced around the square and spotted at least eight FBI agents in various guises. Then a man approached the car, looked in the window and hurried away. This was repeated three times. I know he had a gun, because every time this happened, his hand would slide into his coat.

Eventually he opened the door and slid in beside me. Still very nervous, still looking in all directions, he asked out of the corner of his mouth, 'Are you the English cop they call the Grey Fox?'

I nodded, and he told me that he had been a member of The Syndicate before coming to America. He paused and then he said, 'You know, you won't find Ellul in New York no more. He's moved over to the West Coast — California, I think.'

I asked him how he knew and he said simply, 'He's a friend of mine.'

I pointed out that California was a big state and that Ellul would still take a lot of finding. He shook his head slowly. 'Not that big,' he said, 'when you're looking for a guy with his outlook. He's a big city guy. The small towns and the country would drive him mad. So my guess is that you'll find him holed up in either Los Angeles or Frisco. And it will be in a place where the board is cheap. He's broke.'

I asked the obvious question, 'Why are you telling me all this?'

He smiled for the first time since climbing into the car. He said, 'From the moment they knew you were coming, the cops have been putting the heat on the Maltese community in this city. Maybe if you tell them Philip Ellul's down on the coast, they'll lift the heat.'

There wasn't too much logic in that. No police force is

likely to abandon a search on the basis of a tip-off from an unknown informant. And yet despite his obvious motive, I had a feeling he was telling the truth. If he had wanted to mislead us, he could have made his information sound much more definite.

Our hosts clearly intended to see that no harm befell us during our stay in their city. Several days later, I was due to appear at a radio station. There was a blizzard raging and the roads were blocked. The journey had to be made by subway. So we were given two armed FBI men as escorts, because of the mugging problem in the city. And we only had to travel through three stations!

On our last but one day, we were having lunch in our hotel when a little man joined us, a pleasant character. He introduced himself as the editor of *Inside Detective* and asked whether we would mind if he published a picture of Ellul. I agreed willingly enough; and in due time, I'd have good reason to be glad that I did.

This was the story he printed under the heading, *Are you this man or have you seen him?*:

'We have been asked by Detective Chief Superintendent Albert S. Wickstead of New Scotland Yard's Serious Crimes Squad for assistance in locating the man pictured above. He is 47-year-old Philip Aloysius Ellul, identified as a "vital" witness to a 17-year-old murder of a London gangster. It is believed that Ellul's testimony could help bring down the reign of a ring of London criminals known as "The Syndicate," who control prostitution in the city. Ellul left London in 1969 and Superintendent Wickstead's sources put the man in Colorado that year and in New York City in 1970. He is known to use the aliases Philip Gatt and Philip Buhagian, among others. If you know the whereabouts of Ellul, who reportedly had wanted to contact Wickstead, phone the New York City police intelligence unit which is working with Yard officials in attempting to track him down (Area Code 212-924-7334).'

We had been shown much kindness during our brief stay and wanted to show our appreciation. So after handing out a batch of Metropolitan Police badges as official gifts, we laid on some more personal presents for the men we'd worked alongside.

When Dan Guiney came into his office on our final day, there was a bottle of Scotch whisky (his favourite tipple) standing on his desk. We had wrapped two blue ribbons around it. He didn't say a word. He sank on to his knees, bowed his head and put his hands together.

I said, 'Dan, what are you doing down there?'

'Well,' he said, 'I must be thankful, because I must have pleased either His Holiness or the leprechauns or some other stupid bastard who's left me a bottle of Scotch whisky tied up in blue ribbon.'

That was Lieutenant Dan Guiney. A very nice man. I liked him a lot.

CHAPTER SEVENTEEN

ODD HAPPENINGS AT THE OLD BAILEY

'You tell that Wickstead he won't live to see the end of the trial.' A threat reported by fellow officers.

It was 18 September 1974, the opening day of The Syndicate's vice trial. The eleven defendants were already in the dock. Bewigged counsel were seated alongside a formidable array of documents. And everyone was awaiting the arrival of the judge, Mr Justice Geoffrey Lane. This was the moment when Silver's solicitor – or should I say ex-solicitor? – chose to make his entry. Silver had changed his solicitors to avoid a conflict of evidence during the trial. As if he had all the time in the world, the solicitor strolled over to the dock and shook the hand of each defendant in turn – although officially he only represented one of them, Victor Micallef. To me, that gesture set the pattern for the entire trial. Relationships between the prosecution and the defence at times became very strained. Many of the traditional courtesies were waived. And all in all, some very strange things would occur along the way.

Our problem, as always in a case involving organised crime, had been that of finding and keeping our witnesses.

Just seven days earlier, Bernard Tighe and Stan Clegg had flown to Malta and made arrangements for the witnesses in the vice trial to travel to England. But when I rang Inspector Fred Calleja of the Malta Police to tell him about the new situation, he told me that everything had changed.

Most of our witnesses had succumbed to a mixture of threats and bribes. The Serious Crime Squad were no longer welcome on the island. And Fred, a steadfastly loyal friend to us, had himself been prevented from speaking to certain witnesses and ordered to return to uniform duty.

On Monday, 16 September, the murder trial concerning Tommy Smithson was called before Mr Justice Geoffrey Lane at the Old Bailey. But before the indictment was put, Michael Corkery, the senior Treasury Counsel who was prosecuting in this case, made application that the trial should be postponed on the grounds that the witnesses had been bribed and intimidated. In support of this application, Fred Calleja and Bernie Tighe went into the witness box to give first-hand accounts of these events in Malta. Fred also told the judge that a five-figure contract had been placed upon my head. Two Maltese hit-men had left the island and it was believed that they had already arrived in England. Fellow officers told of another threat made to them in these words: 'You tell that Wickstead he won't live to see the end of the trial. And if we can't get him we will get his kids.' The judge immediately ruled that the murder trial should be postponed indefinitely — and that the vice trial should commence in two days' time. He asked me how long I would need to prove conclusively that our witnesses had been bribed and intimidated. I told him that I couldn't put a definite time limit on this, but I thought it could be achieved within three weeks.

With this target in mind, Ken Tolbart and Roger Stoodley flew out to San Francisco in search of Ellul, while Bernie Tighe, John Lewis and Geordie Corner went to Malta, the island where we were no longer welcome.

Since taking command of the Serious Crime Squad, threats had become very much part of my life; and hitherto I had never taken them too seriously. Gangsters, villains, etc., tend to be vainglorious. When under pressure, certainly when about to fall, they like to make the defiant gesture. It encourages their followers to believe that they're not really beaten after all, that they will still have the last word. However, most of these threats made against police officers are just bombast and bluster.

But now, for the first time, I was prepared to take a threat seriously. Fred Calleja's information came from a reliable source. And considering that we were in the process of toppling a multi-million pound empire, there was nothing very remarkable about a five-figure contract. When faced with this kind of situation, there can only be one response. You shrug it aside. As a police officer, you mustn't take one backward step. If you do, where do you stop? You'll be walking backwards for the rest of your life.

I did have a guard placed upon my wife and upon my sons. And I took what I considered to be sensible precautions. I varied my route to work each day and I also varied my time schedules. But I didn't feel that I needed a personal guard. My squad clearly thought otherwise.

When shopping in the local supermarket, I rounded the line of shelves and literally bumped into one of my own men. I was mildly surprised, because I had never seen him there before. Out on the street, I spotted another of my off-duty officers – and again this wasn't his part of London. If I went for a drink, there always seemed to be someone eager to keep me company. I might have wondered about this new-found popularity.

134

But, of course, by then I had come to understand. My squad had decided to look after me in their own way. I couldn't have been in better hands.

Still, even if the contract had been carried out and they had removed me, it wouldn't have made the slightest difference. The evidence was all neatly documented. Someone else would have taken my place. And the squad would have been more determined than ever to succeed.

After a few weeks, my wife asked for the guards to be taken away. The sight of policemen in front of the house day after day had created a pressure of its own — a constant reminder of danger. So the guards were taken away. But if she is reading this, she will be learning for the first time that really we only went through the motions. We still kept the house under observation. We were just a bit more discreet about it, that's all. I had no wish to see her brought down under pressure.

Once the trial had commenced, the well of the court had the look of a legal *Who's Who*. Bernard Silver had Richard Lowry Q.C. as his counsel. Tony Mangion had Kenneth Machin Q.C.; Victor Micallef had Sir Dingle Foot (brother of Michael); Frank Melito had William Hemming Q.C.; Emmanuel Bartolo had Sir Harold Cassels Q.C.; and so it went. A very formidable array.

But there was one man in the well of the court who appeared to be a strange bedfellow for the rest of this legal brigade. He was a Soho frequenter and friend and associate of the men in the dock. Some of the witnesses for the prosecution, both male and female, had reason to fear him. You can imagine how they would feel when they stepped into the box and found him facing them from a distance of about three yards. The Metropolitan Police had no jurisdiction at the Old Bailey. So I asked the court ushers and the City of London police to remove him. However, it was then discovered that he was employed by a solicitor for the duration of the trial as a runner.

I spoke to Michael Corkery and he immediately approached the judge, taking Sir Dingle Foot with him.

As a result of this meeting, the judge directed that he should be banned from the well of the court – but added that he could, if he so wished, go into the public gallery. Despite the most persistent protestations from the solicitor, this was done.

This proved to be little more than a hint of things to come. Normally by the time you reach the Old Bailey, you expect the chicanery to end. But during this trial, strange things continued to occur, both in the cells and on the floor of the court itself. My squad and I needed sharp eyes and sharp ears in the days that followed. One afternoon, for instance, I learned that a prisoner had been visited in his cell beneath the court by two men during the official visiting period. And there in the shadow of that famous statue of justice, they had agreed to give false evidence on his behalf. Before that night was over, I had seen the two men. They admitted that an approach had been made to them, adding hastily that they wanted no part in it. They made full statements and then repeated those statements from the witness box the following day, in spite of vigorous assertions from defence counsel that it was a fresh offence of conspiracy and shouldn't be brought into the present case.

Later a much more elaborate plot was hatched by the various defendants. They decided that while giving evidence in their own defence, they would 'accidentally' mention the murder of Tommy Smithson and the forthcoming murder trial. This would have resulted in the immediate stoppage of the present trial, followed by a re-trial. Michael Corkery was told by one of his defence colleagues and he in turn informed the judge, whereupon all counsel in the case were addressed. As a result, the defendants were brought before the judge and told that he knew about the conspiracy. He warned them that no matter what they might say, and no matter what disclosures were made about other indictments and trials, there would be no re-trial.

The odd happenings continued.

Our Soho frequenter was seen to lean over the edge of

the public gallery and speak to one of the defendants who had been waiting to re-enter the dock during a court recess. This time the judge, patience exhausted, banned him from the court precincts during the duration of the trial.

A solicitor (not connected with the defence, but a witness in the case) had files in his possession which gave details of properties owned by The Syndicate in the Soho area. The solicitor, incidentally, had said that he didn't know any of The Syndicate. He was ordered to bring these files to court. The judge took this a stage further by directing that he should be taken to his business premises by officers of my squad, so that they could check the existence of all such documents. He duly brought the files to the Old Bailey. At the close of the day's proceedings, the judge instructed him to hand them over to the police while still within the court's precincts. After the judge and jury had left, the solicitor remained seated in the well of the court – and Joyce Cashmore noticed that he was slipping certain documents under a manilla folder. He was also seen to fold an envelope and place it between his knees, so that it didn't show. She brought this to my attention. I allowed five minutes to elapse before taking action, to see whether he made any attempt to retrieve the envelope. Then I uncovered the documents from beneath the manilla folder. They bore the heading 'Soho Group' with the names of some of the defendants thereon. I also took the envelope, still gripped between his knees – and he gave the lame excuse that it must have fallen off the table. The envelope bore, in his own handwriting, the private telephone number of Bernard Silver and the Dublin address of Frank Mifsud.

Owing to the length and magnitude of the trial, counsel were in the habit of leaving their papers on their desks in court overnight. One morning, Geordie Corner arrived early at the Old Bailey and discovered a solicitor's representative looking at the papers on Michael Corkery's rostrum. He ejected him from the court and informed Mr Corkery. The clerk was asked to explain his actions. He said that he was still a student of the law and anxious to study the way in which various counsel put their cases. In particular, he had wanted to see the kind of index used by Treasury Counsel. Michael Corkery accepted the explanation and this underlined a very nice aspect of his character. He liked to believe the best of all men.

I suppose the event which disturbed me most during the trial was the giving of evidence by three senior police officers (two of them retired) on Bernie Silver's behalf. They had been served with subpoenas and thus had no choice. They had to appear. They said that they had known him for periods ranging from fifteen to twenty-six years. He had never been a violent man; and as far as they knew, he had no involvement with vice whatsoever. Well, like Michael Corkery, I wish to believe the best of all men – but this I found very hard to accept. Later, Silver admitted that he had operated pornographic bookshops in Soho and the West End for a number of years. It was common knowledge throughout the underworld that Silver was one of the controlling forces in West End vice. And certain areas of Soho were frequently referred to by the press as 'Silver City.' Subsequent to this trial, an M.P. put down the following question for the Home Secretary: 'Whether he will draw up and publish regulations governing the giving of evidence by senior Metropolitan Police officers on behalf of persons charged with serious criminal offences.'

That evening, the Commissioner of the Metropolitan Police Sir Robert Mark, the Assistant Commissioner Colin Woods and the Deputy Assistant Commissioner Ernie Bond came to my office in Limehouse to discuss this turn of events. Their feelings echoed my own and it was the only time I ever heard Robert Mark swear. He was normally the most equable of men and, in my opinion, the best Commissioner the Met ever had. He had arrived at a very opportune moment in its history. The Met had been in danger of losing its good name. It wasn't as honest as it had once been; not as dedicated and consequently not as successful in the pursuit of criminals. But from the moment of his arrival, he made his position crystal clear. Corruption wouldn't be tolerated in any shape or form. It would be weeded out ruthlessly. But if a man was prepared to work hard and honestly for the force, he would back him every step along the way. His loyalty would be total. I know, because that's the kind of loyalty he gave to me.

One of the more pleasant incidents in the trial came with the arrival of a Chinese gentleman named James Hing. He was wearing white canvas shoes, white drill trousers and the most spectacular silk shirt in rainbow hues – and he was asking for me. I went to see him and he told me that he had read about the trial in his newspaper in Guyana. Wanting to give evidence against The Syndicate, he had stepped on the very next plane to England. Just like that. Four thousand miles. Straight from a Caribbean summer to the start of an English winter – and without even taking time out to change his clothes.

He had a burning sense of injustice, and with good cause. He told me how he and his wife and children had occupied a flat in Soho above a strip club. The Syndicate had tried to buy him out, but he had refused. They threatened him, but he still refused to move. So in the end, they chopped away the stairs. It was then that, fearing for the safety of his wife and children, he finally gave up and left the country. He made a full statement and was allowed to give his evidence the next day which was particularly damaging to the case of Tony Mangion. And I am very glad to say that the judge then ruled that his air fare should be repaid – as a reward for his courage and public-spirited attitude.

The trial finally ended after sixty-five exhausting working days. The defendants, Bernie Silver, Tony Mangion, Emmanuel Bartolo, Frank Melito, Victor Micallef and others were found guilty of conspiracy to live on immoral earnings. Silver was sentenced to six years imprisonment, Mangion and Bartolo to five, Melito to four, and Micallef to three. The Syndicate had been broken and I was filled with a great sense of relief. Since the start of this trial, because of its complexity and ramifications, I had been very conscious of the effect it would have on the Police Service. For the first time I felt old and tired, and probably looked it too.

However, it was very satisfying to hear the judge make this remark in praise of the Serious Crime Squad: 'It is quite obvious in this case to anyone who has sat through it that the amount of work done by the police and the extent of their enquiries has been quite extraordinary. Insofar as it may lie outside their line of duty, they are to be congratulated for what they have done.'

But perhaps my most lasting memory of that final day was provided by Bernie Silver. Upon being sentenced, he turned, cool and composed as ever, and gave me a mock bow. Did that gesture signify grudging respect or continued defiance or maybe a mixture of both? Only Bernie Silver could know.

CHAPTER EIGHTEEN

GHOST OF SCARFACE

'I got to be very much a loner. I don't like this continual company.' Philip 'The Malt' Ellul explaining why he didn't wish to be guarded.

From a distance of four thousand miles, the voice of Philip Ellul sounded more American than Maltese. He was saying, 'I understand you wish to see me.'

This could have ranked as one of the understatements of the year. I told him, 'Yes, I do. Because I believe you are now willing to tell me the full story behind Tommy Smithson's murder.'

He said that he was — but sensing the hesitancy, I added, 'The Syndicate leaders are now in custody and awaiting trial. This is why I need your testimony, why I want you to come to England.'

'If I do,' he asked, 'will there be any further charges laid against me?'

I told him, 'You've served your time. You will be free to come and go as you wish.' The Home Office had given permission as he was still on licence.

Suddenly all hesitancy was gone. 'All right. Which flight shall I catch?'

I said flatly, 'You don't. You stay where you are. I'm sending two of my men to escort you. From now on, we're looking after you.'

Ken Tolbart and John Farley flew out on the first available flight to America and duly returned with Ellul. My visit to New York had paid dividends at last and I had good cause to bless the editor of *True Detective* who'd printed a picture of the one-time hit man. An avid reader of the magazine had spotted Ellul on a park bench in San Francisco. He told the city police, who immediately detained him and put the phone call through to me at Limehouse. Ellul was, of course, a vital witness. So much of the other evidence we'd gathered could have been described as hearsay. But as the man convicted of Smithson's murder, Ellul was in the unique position of being able to name the men who had taken out the contract. Over seventeen years had gone by since that June day in 1956 when Smithson had been shot to death in a Kilburn flat, but I was determined to see that his ghost haunted The Syndicate.

Smithson had been a small-time gangster with big dreams. His speciality was to demand protection money from strip clubs and gambling clubs. As such establishments were mostly controlled by criminals more powerful than himself, the risk was obvious. He was even rash enough to try to muscle in upon the empire of Billy Hill. As a consequence, he was twice beaten very badly. In fact, beatings for Tommy Smithson were to become a way of life. Throughout his brief and violent career, he was either carrying out attacks on other men or being attacked himself.

On one occasion, he had been kidnapped and hustled off Chicago-style, in a car, by a gang of men. His unconscious body was later dumped while the car was still in motion. Fifty-four stitches were required to patch up his face. In true gangland tradition, he refused to name his attackers. To show that all was forgiven, a party was thrown in his honour. That was how he picked up the name of Scarface. But there was something strangely euphoric about Tommy Smithson. He just continued to move along his chosen course, seemingly oblivious to the risks he ran. A self-destructive fellow who was doomed, by his very nature, to die young. In the end, it was the mysterious Fay Sadler, our missing witness in the Pen Club murder case, who unwittingly brought about his destruction. She was his mistress and he was infatuated by her. Now this was one of the odd things about Fay Sadler which had always puzzled me. She couldn't have been described as a beautiful woman by any stretch of the imagination. When she spoke, there was no outward sign of any great wit, warmth, intelligence or charm. Yet she did have the most devastating effect upon the men in her life – so there must have been something special about the lady. They were seemingly prepared to do anything to protect her. When she ran into some minor trouble with the law, Smithson's reaction was predictable. He set out to raise a fund for her legal defence, and decided that The Syndicate should make the major contribution. His collection methods were rough. When George Caruana showed a certain reluctance to pay, Smithson flew into a rage and attacked him with a knife. Caruana protected his face with his hands, and both hands were badly cut.

Smithson then confronted Frank Mifsud in the presence of some of his minions. This move was described in underworld circles as 'putting the arm on Big Frank' – and from Smithson's point of view, the timing couldn't have been worse. The Syndicate were just about to advance into the West End in their bid to take over the empire of the Messinas. At this stage, they couldn't afford to show the slightest sign of weakness.

Smithson already knew his eventual killers, Ellul and Spampinato. They had accompanied him on various violent forays and acted as hatchet men on his behalf. He had even had breakfast with Spampinato three weeks before his death, when they were on the friendliest of terms.

Ellul was a stocky man, wide of shoulder, deep of chest, but he was dwarfed by Spampinato, a very menacing figure of a man. He understood the law well enough to realise that, having been declared not guilty of Smithson's murder, he was immune from further prosecution on that count. So some years later, he sold his story to a Sunday newspaper. His taped interview with the reporter, John Lisners, was handed to Scotland Yard. Spampinato admitted freely that Ellul and himself had been given the contract to kill Smithson, with the message: 'This punk has got to be exterminated.' They stalked him for days and eventually caught up with their man in a boarding house at Carlton Vale, Kilburn. Ellul had a gun and Spampinato a knife.

Smithson was in an upstairs room with a girl, and this is how Spampinato described what followed: 'Just before we walked into the room, Philip said: "He's my pigeon. Leave him to me." Tommy said hello to us. Philip just growled like a tiger. He pulled the automatic from his jacket, slides the breach and goes bang. The bullet went right through his arm.'

At that point, the gun jammed. After a struggle with the mechanism, Ellul cleared the gun and fired a second shot which hit Smithson in the neck.

Spampinato takes up the story again.

'Blood started coming out. Thick blood like liver, from his mouth. This man, I thought, has had it. Mission accomplished. I was really enjoying myself.'

After reading that, do you wonder that policemen such as I sometimes despair of a society that seems so anxious to forgive the violent criminal and forget the victim? I have interviewed and spoken to many a murderer and violent gangster and always I got the same replies that 'life is cheap these days because the law has made it cheap'. All the deterrents to violence have been removed: the death penalty; corporal punishment. The villains don't have to think about this anymore. They go out on their jobs, armed and in a state of mind to kill if necessary. They will receive no extra punishment for it.

I become very bitter when I read of the efforts made on behalf of the poor misunderstood criminal. What about the victim? I would dearly like to see these do-gooders attend a mortuary and a post mortem, and most of all, I'd like to make them try and comfort grieving relatives and friends. Who knows? It might make them realise what life, and death, is really all about.

Still, leaving that aside, Spampinato was obviously a vital witness. His 'contract' hadn't been honoured and he was just as bitter as Ellul. When my officers caught up with him in Malta, he was unemployed and following a precarious existence as a wine-bar tout. He gave us a very valuable statement and after some persuasion agreed to attend Old Street magistrates' court for the commital proceedings. He arrived at Heathrow at six o'clock one morning, was brought immediately to my office, had breakfast and was taken straight into court.

I shall never forget the effect his appearance had upon the defendants. No one, except my squad and prosecuting counsel, knew that he was due to appear. Mr David Tudor-Price, now a senior Old Bailey judge, stood up and in slow, deliberate tones, called out, 'Mr Spampinato, please.'

The faces in and around the dock were a picture. Silver suddenly looked very strained. Bartolo, the comedian of the gang, went white, the blood draining from his face. Tony Mangion's head bowed and they all seemed equally thunderstruck.

Spampinato walked into court, heavy featured and unshaven after his journey. He was dressed in black, the age-old colour of menace. And throughout his evidence, he stared straight at the prisoners. His attitude to them was clear. 'There it is, do what the hell you like!'

His evidence couldn't have been more dramatic. When he spoke about the murder in that gravelly voice of his, the court room became even quieter than usual. But throughout this case, we were constantly to be reminded that we were opposed by a multi-million pound empire. The Syndicate had the power to buy any but the most honest of men. And there cannot be any real doubt that they had bought Spampinato. He went back to Malta and enjoyed a sudden change of fortune. The struggling wine bar tout received £30,000, a new car and a brand new villa on the sea-front at Sliema. Needless to say, he didn't keep his promise to us: namely, to return to England and repeat his evidence when The Syndicate appeared at the Old Bailey. He must have felt that there was no need. His contract had been honoured – albeit seventeen years late.

This was why Ellul was so important to us. As far as the conspiracy to murder charge was concerned, he was now our only star witness. We already had his statement. But if our evidence was to be presented properly, we needed his presence in court. We guarded him closely when he first arrived in London. Too closely, as it transpired. After a few days, he was saying, 'Look, I can't stand this close observation. You must understand that I was sentenced to death. I was in the death cell and within forty-eight hours of hanging, and I got to be very much a loner. I don't like this continual company. Would you mind taking it off?'

We agreed a compromise. He was moved into an empty police flat at Limehouse and given a small allowance. He spent a large part of each day watching television up there on the third floor. He liked to watch the horse racing and from time to time, he'd visit the betting shop just around the corner. He had always been a gambling man. On occasions, he would decide to go for a walk on his own. There was nothing we could do about that. He was legally free to come and go as he pleased. We had no power to detain him or to control his movements in any way. Naturally we still kept him under observation. But this is a well-nigh impossible task unless you have the full co-operation of the subject. You can't watch a man twenty-four hours a day indefinitely – particularly a man as streetwise as Ellul. Clearly some day, somehow, he made contact with The Syndicate, or they with him. He told us that he wished to return to the States, as there were various matters to be attended to.

He promised to return in time for the trial and once again the promise wasn't kept. We later learned that his silence had been bought with £60,000. Now the other half of the contract had been honoured.

Far be it for me to complain. That is not my province. But just the same, in the face of that I did sometimes wish that someone would tell me just how I could hope to find honest witnesses in the kind of world in which I worked.

CHAPTER NINETEEN

RETURN OF BIG FRANK

'I control the West End and the West End police.'
Claim by Frank Mifsud.

The big plane sat on the runway at Heathrow, silent and almost deserted. The passengers had left and only Frank Mifsud remained, guarded by his escorting officers, Terry Brown and Stanley Clegg. He was slumped in his seat, head down, his hair grey, thin and unruly. The suit was surprisngly shabby for a millionaire. As I came down the gangway, he raised his head briefly, looking at me with vacant eyes, then his chin returned once more to his chest. The portrait of a broken man. For Big Frank Mifsud, vice czar of Soho, the running was over. On the night when we raided the Scheherazade, he had received a mysterious phone call at his Dublin home and promptly set off on a ten-thousand mile trail that led through South America, France and Austria to Switzerland, where he was finally arrested.

I arrested him formally and he didn't reply. I asked him whether he understood and he mumbled something – his voice pitched so low that it was difficult to hear. I was wondering how anyone could ever have feared such a man. Remember, this was the man who had imposed a rule of terror over Soho for two decades, the man who had once boasted, 'I control the West End and the West End police.'

But then, of course, money is power in the underworld. When you couple that with the ruthlessness Mifsud possessed during the fifties and sixties, you had genuine grounds for fear. He had bands of small-time criminals, anxious to obey his every command. As one of his minions told us, 'If Big Frank told you to do something, there would be no question about it. You wouldn't even ask for money. You thought he might pay you some day. But even if he didn't, you respected him and wanted to get his attention.' His appearance helped build up his reputation as a frightener – eighteen stone, cold eyes and black rages. So too did the rumour that he was on friendly terms with the Kray twins and other London gangs versed in violence. Certainly, if someone displeased him, he wouldn't hesitate to have the offender badly beaten. But this would always be done by somebody else, and so didn't require any show of courage on Mifsud's part. Even in his Brick Lane days, I never heard an instance of him being engaged in personal violence.

As a man, he didn't impress me at all. He was too full of self-pity, too ready to crumble under pressure. I had little time for his fellow boss, Bernie Silver, but at least he'd shown a certain amount of grit when the going got tough. We handcuffed Mifsud to take him from the plane to the waiting car, simply because this is routine when transporting a man in custody. However, it seemed an empty gesture. I have rarely seen a prisoner who appeared less likely to make a bid for freedom.

As our car threaded its way through the traffic and towards Limehouse, he told me that he'd changed. 'I am very much a family man now,' he said. 'That is all I live for, all I want – the thing I miss most.' He also talked about the thousands of pounds he had supposedly given to charity. 'I have the receipts to prove it,' he said. But for most of the journey, he remained silent, sunk in gloom, very much aware of the fact that at long last his luck had run out. He had climbed high (financially at least) from traffic cop to merchant seaman to builder to vice czar millionaire. He had developed a taste for the luxuries of life. And so the past few months must have had a sobering effect. For a while, he had lived in a small tent on the Austria-Swiss border. This perilous freedom came to an end when he moved into a hotel in Olten, Switzerland. He was arrested. Then he somehow contrived to get himself transferred to a private mental hospital in Solothurn, a mountain township lying at the base of snowclad mountains about seventy miles from Zurich. He claimed that he was too sick to be extradited. The Swiss authorities thought otherwise. Even an appeal by his Swiss lawyer to the European Human Rights Commission in Strasbourg, on the grounds of ill health, was rejected. Hence his arrival at Heathrow.

In addition to a murder charge, Mifsud also faced a charge of suborning a witness to commit perjury in a case which went back seven years. This related to a feud that had developed between Mifsud and Tony Cauci, another club owner. They had once been on friendly terms. But when Cauci bought a strip club in Soho called The Carnival, attitudes changed. As Cauci put it, 'This caused the bad blood between us.' Silver and Mifsud jointly owned nineteen of the twenty-four strip clubs which were operating in the area, and bitterly resented the presence of rivals. Around the close of 1966 and the beginning of 1967, there were petrol-bomb explosions at three of Mifsud's more profitable ventures, the Gigi in Frith Street, the Keyhole in Old Compton Street and a gaming club in Greek Street. Mifsud appeared to be convinced that Cauci was responsible for the bombings. Eventually Cauci and his doorman, Derek Galea, were charged with conspiracy in connection with the Greek Street explosion. Harold Stocker, who ran a hot-dog stall in Soho, stated that he had seen Galea running from the club immediately after it burst into flames. Galea then gave evidence against Cauci, his boss. Cauci was jailed for five years and Galea for two.

But during my investigations into The Syndicate, I learned that Stocker had given perjured evidence at the trial upon the instructions of Mifsud – and that Galea, although a co-defendant, had likewise committed perjury.

When interviewed, they admitted this freely. Stocker said that he had been promised one hundred pounds, but had only received fifteen. Galea had been given one hundred pounds, after his release, and set up in a coffee shop in Wardour Mews. Both said they had committed perjury because they were terrified of Big Frank.

I found Tony Cauci, not surprisingly, a bitter, hate-filled man. His entire body had been fashioned in curves. He was a Buddha with a cast in one eye, perhaps, at first glance, a man not to be taken too seriously. But just the same, he was one of the very few men in Soho brave enough to stand firm against Mifsud and The Syndicate. And when he went into the witness box at Mifsud's trial, he remained equally firm. He became angry, yes, but his evidence never wavered.

Mifsud was acquitted on the murder charge, but was found guilty on the perjury issue and sentenced to five years in jail. Subsequently three Appeal Court judges quashed the sentence – ruling that the jury had been allowed to hear inadmissible evidence from Galea.

It was perhaps a good moment for me to remember the words of Edmund Burke: 'I am not determining a point of law; I am restoring tranquillity.'

Frank Mifsud had regained his freedom, but he personally would never again pose a threat to Soho. Under the terms of his extradition document he had three weeks' liberty before we could prefer other charges. He well knew that we could and would do this, and he hurriedly left the country to live on the proceeds of his numbered Swiss bank accounts. Now that The Syndicate had been broken, the streets of London would be a little more tranquil than before.

CHAPTER TWENTY

THE LAST DAY

'I'm going straight. It's a lot less bother.' Ruby Sparks.

It was 20 December 1977, the day of my retirement party. The end of a career that had spanned over thirty years. The start of a new life that I regarded with mixed feelings.

Certainly I was looking forward to spending time with my wife and my boys. there was a lot of catching up to do. And I was very tired, very much in need of a change. Command of the Serious Crime Squad had taken its toll. The job is so demanding, so all-consuming, that a few years can seem like a lifetime.

But there were other aspects of retirement that worried me. I had never had the time, or, frankly, the inclination, to mix socially. My only real interests lay in police work and the ever-changing fortunes of West Ham United. I had no small talk and I very much doubted whether I could change my ways. Nearly all my close friends were policemen. And now I had come to say goodbye to all those friends – in no way sure that I would find any new ones.

As I looked around the room, they were all there, the friends and colleagues who had peopled my life for the past thirty years.

The top brass were represented by Gilbert Kelland, the Assistant Commissioner, Crime. A very straight, very honest, very decent man who had been a staunch friend to me in times of trouble. Ron Steventon, Deputy

Assistant Commissioner, Crime. We had been aides to CID on adjoining Divisions, had attended selection boards together. A man who was steeped in police tradition, ever ready to assist a colleague and most of all a very valued friend. Trevor Lloyd Hughes and Mike Taylor from my last squad. Both now Commanders, excellent police officers, of great value to the service, and again good friends. John McCammont who was later to leave the Met. and become a provincial Detective Chief Inspector. Not forgetting, of course, my excellent colleagues from the Hertfordshire Force, Ron Harvey, Tony Hill, Bert Peters and Ken Morris.

Senior Treasury Counsel were present in the very welcome form of Michael Corkery, David Tudor-Price and Michael Hill.

Equally welcome were the City Police who had been so good to me on all those occasions when I'd been at the Old Bailey, and during the previous twelve years, it must have seemed as though I had taken up permanent residence at those famous courts. I was never more honoured than when I was made a Freeman of the City of London, sponsored by Sir Carl Aarvold, the then Recorder of London sitting at the Old Bailey, and the keeper of that establishment, Jack Gamble, a man I am pleased to have known and to call a friend. Many years later he joined me in a conspiracy whereby the same Freedom of the City was conferred on my dear wife. My two sons who were present thought the highlight of the proceedings was the roast beef lunch that followed in Jack's quarters at the Old Bailey!

Particularly pleasing to me was the sight of the entire Serious Crime Squad.

The goodwill messages came from far afield: from the FBI: from Fred Calleja in Malta: from the excellent Joe Mountsey of the Lancashire Constabulary (whom I'd met during the Sewell case); and, of course, from Scotland Yard. The then Commissioner, Sir David McNee, had thanked me generously for the work I'd done. Former Commissioner Sir Robert Mark sent me a kind letter. And so did the Deputy Commissioner, Sir Colin Woods.

A very treasured letter came from Doylan Williams on behalf of the DPP's office. He said, 'No one who has had the pleasure and the stimulus of working with you will fail to feel a certain sadness that even you must go from the Service. As for me, I shall never forget the personal warmth you showed me, no matter what the problem might be.' And then he added in brackets: 'Is there always a crisis going on?' I liked that, because in our combined jobs there had indeed always been a crisis. But the important thing to remember was that during those trauma-filled days, he and his colleagues had always been there to turn to – and they'd always found the time to listen and to help.

I had one very pleasant surprise. I'd previously asked whether I could purchase my office chair at Limehouse. It was comfortable and I'd become accustomed to it. But I was told, no, it wasn't on. The Service didn't allow it. Used to be the custom, but not any more. Anyway, lo and behold at the party, my very good friend Ron Steventon, now DAC Admin, presented me with the chair, complete with its new brass plate. Ron, who knew me rather better than most, had doubtless reasoned that my desire for that chair was largely a sentimental one. And Ron could well have been right.

There were a lot of speeches, all very kind, and then it was my turn to speak. And do you know, it was impossible. I was suddenly terribly conscious of the fact that this really was goodbye. No more. This is the end. Your service is finished.

I had planned out my speech a dozen times or more. And now that the time had come, all I could say was, 'Thank you ... thank you very much.' A little on the brief side, but at least you can be sure of one thing: I meant it. And there were tears in my eyes to prove it.

However, as I come to the last pages of my book, I realise that I was wrong that day. The story itself hasn't really ended at all. There is no finality, no ultimate conclusion, no last chapter that abruptly severs the strings of a lifetime. I suppose that I of all people should have remembered that the police look after their own, that the bonds of comradeship and friendship forged under fire couldn't be broken by a mere retirement. Nor could I simply shrug aside the past as though it had never been. Even today, I still follow the fortunes of old colleagues and one-time criminal opponents with more than a passing interest.

I know, for instance, that Frank Mifsud and most of the original Syndicate leaders are back in their Maltese homeland, living in luxury.

Quite by chance, I spotted Bernie Silver strolling through the West End. He looked older and greyer than of yore, and the spring had gone from his step. But then maybe the years are catching up with us all.

Norma Levy still catches the headlines as she battles with the state authorities for the right to remain in Miami. She has no wish to return to London. She says she would miss the Florida sunshine.

The last time I heard of Fay Sadler, she was married, reformed and setting out for Australia in a bid to make a fresh start. I hope she made it.

Ruby Sparks (I wonder if he is still alive), dry as ever, declared many moons ago, 'I'm going straight. It's a lot less bother.' And somehow I think that Ruby would have been a little disenchanted with many of his modern-day counterparts. Women and children were never his targets, nor was mindless violence his game.

And although the original Serious Crime Squad has been disbanded and scattered, they are still my friends, still very much part of my life. When we meet up, which is often, the old battles are refought. Yesterday becomes today. And we return once more to the twilight world.

INDEX

156